Uniquely You
Pulling off the Mask

LaSandra Collins

WP
WALTON

DEDICATION

To all those struggling with their spiritual identity seeking to find their purpose in the Kingdom, I know how you feel, I have been there, and this book is dedicated to you!

FOREWORDS

"Your latter will be greater…"

LaSandra Collins is an average person whom God has chosen to use beyond measure. She's a down-home girl, whose voice as a powerful woman is exuberantly unique for the purpose of assisting the masses in identifying who they are and assisting them with removing the negative masks that affect them as people.

LaSandra shares pivotal points in her life from childhood to adulthood, unmasking pain, trust, grief, self-love, marital problems, heartache, and more – all while working every adversity; later realizing through God's grace and mercy that none of it was without purpose. LaSandra not only takes us on her own walk, but giftedly prepares one for their own personal unique un-masking. From down in the trenches to the successful woman she is today, LaSandra paints a powerful story of what perseverance looks like, when God is in control.

LaTonya White (#TVmaTheTea)

Motivational Speaker, TV Host, Entrepreneur, and Blogger

I am extremely excited and thrilled to write this foreword. It gives me great pleasure to share my thoughts regarding LaSandra Collins' book, "Uniquely You: Pulling off the Mask".

As a film director, it is important for me to send positive messages into the universe. These messages should reflect a person's ability to freely share their true experiences. We know this is not an easy task to achieve, because too many people are afraid of what others would think about them if their secrets were exposed. Nonetheless, LaSandra Collins' book, "Uniquely You" explores the stages in her life, while hiding behind a mask. She writes about the entrapment she experienced in her childhood, which spilled into her adult life. This entrapment became a recipe for fail relationships and produced thoughts of not being "good enough".

In an effort to free her mind and life from this destructive behavior, she had to quickly make a decision to take off her masks to follow freedom, or to continue on a road of wearing multiple self-destructive masks. However, we are not any different from LaSandra. In fact, the problem is, we do not have the courage to look inward at our weaknesses and fears. Instead, we wear our masks and point fingers at others.

"Uniquely You: Pulling off the Mask," helped me to explore my various masks I wear daily. After reading Mrs. Collins' book, I have been given the courage to unveil my masks with grace and ease. I have learned the gift of forgiveness.

Arlene Russell

Film Director

In the openly honest book, "Uniquely You – Pulling Off the Mask" LaSandra Collins tells a powerful recap of the many adversaries she faced, starting at the early age of five, that led her to a life of hiding behind many layers of masks. LaSandra takes you on a journey of healing and discovery through self-reflection and the realization that God had purpose in her path. Prepare to "get real" with yourself! In this thought-provoking book, LaSandra will have you answering the tough questions that have you hiding behind the masks that prevent you from the life God has in store for you. LaSandra will show you how to pull off your mask and live the Christ filled life you deserve!

Christi Finnell

The Woodlands Finest Realty Group, The Woodlands, TX

ACKNOWLEDGEMENTS

To my Priest, Protector, and Provider, Kelvin Collins. You are my rock. As I think about what you and I have been through over the past 24 years, I cannot help but thank God for you. From the bottom of my heart, I thank you for your unwavering support. Thank you for not getting upset when I kept you up at night because I could not sleep. Thank you for reading every single chapter after I completed it and providing me feedback. More importantly, thank you for being okay, and understanding my purpose and the "Why" in writing this book. I am sure every wife feels like she has the best husband in her corner, but I can say unequivocally, you are the absolute best husband a woman could ask for. In you, I have what God knew I needed and not what I wanted. I love you infinity times infinity times infinity!

To Shaunda Williams, my sister in Christ, my best friend, confidant, and prayer partner! The Bible says, "For there is a friend that sticks closer than a brother" (Proverbs 18:24). I cannot thank you enough for all you have done for me. Thank you for always being there for me through the good, the bad, and the not so good.

To Karla McKissack-Richardson, my sister in Christ, my best friend, and accountability and prayer partner. I can always count on you to keep me not only prayed up but accountable to my commitment. I appreciate the calls and you asking me 'where are you with writing your book and what chapter are you on this week?' I so appreciate you and our friendship; thank you for all that you do.

To my mother, Emma Alexander, and my sisters; Melanie Bazile, Redessa Shaw, and Robin Zierold, my biggest fans! Thank you so much for your love and support! I love you all!

To Dr. Sherrie Walton, where do I start? Thank you so much for your coaching and guidance in bringing this book to life. Who knew when we met at that event that this is what God had in mind? I am forever grateful for you and thank you for your all your help.

Finally, thank you to all of those who kept me lifted in prayer, asked me how the book was going, and read the first few chapters providing feedback. I love and appreciate you all.

TABLE OF CONTENTS

INTRODUCTION

———————— ❃ ————————

No matter what others say about you, you are fearfully and wonderfully made! I know, life experiences have a way of causing us to question our value, self-worth and at times, who we really are. I have experienced many of those moments. There was a time in my life I had even gone as far as to ask myself and others, *"Why am I here; is there more to life than this"* I am not happy about that period in my life. I was in a dark, lonely, and desolate place. I did not know how or who could help me transition out of it, which brings me to why I am writing this book!

I wrote this book for those of you who are like I once was, hiding who you really are to be accepted. For those of you who are holding onto a past hurt and it has incapacitated you. The pain is so deep that you walk around daily dying on the inside. I wrote this for those of you who have mastered living life with a plastered smile on your face to hide your pain. This book is for the person running from your calling – your divine purpose. Whatever your reason is for putting on your mask day in and day out, this book is the antidote!

I know what you are going through. For years, I believed

I had to keep my mask on and wear a façade, pretending everything was okay; when I knew it was not. I once wandered aimlessly in the wilderness, trying to figure out who I was and what my purpose was on Earth. I changed my personality to fit in. For me, it seemed as if life was pointless and everything around me was falling apart. One day, the bottom fell out from under me. That day was a pivotal point with an encounter and intervention with the Holy Spirit. That day I decided to take my mask off.

Here is my promise to you, in this book I will give you pointers on how to take your mask off and help you start being the person Christ is calling you to be. I am going to be very transparent with you about my masks and I am going to challenge you to look within. We are going to laugh and yes, even cry while you dig deep and explore, "how and why" you hid behind the mask. It is my prayer that you repent of anything that no longer serves your growth and purpose, and you will align yourself with Jesus Christ. I pray that you can see yourself as God sees you, just as I had to for myself many years ago. By the time you are done, you are going to be ready to take off your mask and embrace who you are in Christ, and begin to walk in your purpose. After you finish this book, your perspective will be different and so will be you. This book was written to help you understand, you are free to be you, that is, "Uniquely You." You do not have to hide who you are any longer, because you were born to stand out.

I am living proof that if you will open your heart and mind, be honest with yourself, and put in the work, the content in this book will help you. I personally experienced the same steps, to remove my masks. It is because I took these steps to remove my mask years ago, hence able to write this book.

I have learned that one of the greatest things you can ever

do for yourself is accept who you are in Christ. This newness will require a shift and a transformation in your thinking and subsequent actions.

I know you are tired and weary, that is why now is the time for you to take the first step in your healing journey. Are you ready? You do not have to be afraid! I will be with you every step of the way. I know all too well how scary it can be to try something new, but if you take this leap of faith, open your heart and mind, and not only read my book but follow the steps, you will never have to wear another mask again!

You and I are about to embark on a journey together. We are hosting a segment of, "This is your life." You are the spectator and I am the lead actress in this saga. Are you ready? Let's go…

"Being who God called you to be takes courage, strength, and tenacity."

Your sister in Christ,

LaSandra Collins

AM I WORTHY?

As I sit and ponder the value I bring,

I question my existence and the essence of my being.

I am puzzled by the gifts and talents God intended me to use,

I sit on them and hide them, so others have no clue.

As God tells me I am created solely for His purpose,

I deny I hear Him and resolve that I am worthless.

The Holy Spirit reminds me daily of the words God said,

I respond to God not in acceptance but a "No" instead.

With fear of being a failure I tell the Lord;

"Father I disagree for I am not worthy of this assignment you gave me, you see?"

"I did this and I did that, I'm afraid the person You want I could never be."

The Lord takes me by the hand and says, "Child listen to Me, I created you for My purpose and My will shall be done. If only you would trust Me, you would see you are the one."

Those things you say you did I forgave you and remember

no more,

You are the one I purposed for the task you stand before.

I know that this is new to you but just know, I will be with you every step of the way.

For you my child, are worthy and that is why Christ laid down his life and rose up on the third day.

CHAPTER ONE
MY UNFILTERED TRUTH

I do not remember much about my childhood, but I do remember the day the plain clothed officers came to our home to tell my mother that my father had been murdered. My sisters and I were playing in the front yard when the officers walked up to the front door and knocked. My mother invited them in and offered them a seat. I could tell something was wrong by the look on my mother's face as they were speaking. They told her that my father had been shot three times in the chest and one time in the head, execution style- while driving a fare to his destination. After the officers delivered the message, the gentlemen left. My mother sat on the couch crying, holding the three of us. None of us could have imagined that evening my father left for this shift at Yellow Cab that it would be the last time we saw him alive. I was just five years of age when this happened and life as I knew it changed. In the blink of an eye, we went from a two-parent household to a single parent household.

I suppose I could tell you that after my father died, I had a horrible childhood, but that is not the case at all. Although I grew up in a single parent household, my sisters and I had a great childhood. My mother entered the workforce and provided for us as best she could. However, the one thing she could not do was give me the love a father would give a daughter. I later realized this one experience influenced many of the decisions I made in life. That one incident influenced my choices in men, how I related to them, and even my struggle with promiscuity; all of these things can be traced back to this traumatic experience. For a long time, I was not in a good place spiritually and I did not know how to have a healthy relationship with a man. I attribute most of this to the lack of growing up in a household and seeing a loving relationship between a man and a woman. To protect us, my mother never bought any men around us nor did she remarry.

Because I was too young to process and heal from the death of my father, I started reacting to this loss in my early adult years. I remember during my teenage years I experienced periods of time where I could not sleep. I would be up at night crying because I missed my daddy. At the time, my mother would become frustrated with me, I believe it was because she did not understand what was going on. Lord knows I did not know why I was experiencing so much pain. All I knew was my father was not around and I missed him. My father's absence in my life resulted in me not using wise judgment. I engaged in countless of toxic relationships, starting with my son's father. He was my very first romantic relationship and experience with a man.

Mask # 1

I put on my first mask at the age of 16 without realizing it. It is amazing how a painful experience can affect you and cause you to retreat inside yourself, shielding you from others in an effort to prevent them from seeing your pain. My first traumatic experience spiraled into multiple tragic encounters. There is one particular event that happened while I was in high school, that I will never forget. Even if I tried, I would have never imagined things unfolding as they did on that night. One night, my best friend and I went on a double date with two upperclassmen from our high school. My friend had a crush on one of the guys and wanted me to meet his friend, so I agreed to go on the double date. The night started off normal, we laughed and enjoyed each other's company late into the evening. It was getting late and we headed back home in separate cars. My date was following my friend and her date. After a short while the cars came to a stop and I did not recognize where the guys had driven us, but it became obvious they had no plans to take us home. I looked up and saw we were sitting in the parking lot of a motel. Now you can imagine my mind was racing, wondering what was going on. I asked myself, *Why are we here?* It was rumored that other kids from the school would go to that motel to have sex. I had heard the stories about who was spotted there over the weekends, but no one could ever accuse me of being caught at that motel because I was a virgin.

I never really thought about having sex, I had a career plan. Sex was not on my mind that night either, but my curfew was. My mother was very strict and if I missed curfew, I was going to get a butt whooping and be punished for the rest of my life. I demanded my date to take me home.

'I'll take you home after you have sex with me,' he responded.

I was in shock and I'm sure he saw the expression on my face.

'If you do not have sex with me, I am not taking you home, you will have to get home the best way you can,' he said so matter-of-factly.

There were so many thoughts that raced through my mind. I tried to find a way out of having sex with him, but it was dark, and I was not familiar with that area of town – I felt trapped. I had an idea to call my mother, but I did not see a phonebooth. It was just as well because I did not know how I would be able to explain why I was at a motel. I did not see anyone else I knew besides my friend and she had already gone into the room with her date. I felt hopeless and the inevitable happened. Against my will, I was forced to have sex with him, losing my virginity to a total stranger. Afterwards he took me home, walked me to the door, told my mother he had car trouble and apologized to her for getting me home late. He told her it would never happen again, and he was right because I never spoke to him again. I was embarrassed and I felt violated. I never told my mother or anyone else what happened that night. That was the night, I was robbed of my innocence. I put on my mask to cover my embarrassment.

As a child, it was my dream to become a doctor, a neurology surgeon to be exact. I remember my mother taking me to the doctor and while in the elevator, an older gentleman asked me what I wanted to be when I grew up. I told him a neurologist because I wanted to research the causes of migraine headaches. I would often get dilapidating headaches while in high school and wanted to know the cause of them. I stayed diligent in my studies keeping this dream in front of me, determined to see it become a reality.

My childhood dreams were finally coming true! During the spring of 1986, I will never forget going to the mailbox, retrieving the mail, and seeing a letter addressed to me from a college. It was there! My first acceptance letter to Prairie View A & M. and a second one for the Prairie View A & M Nursing School. *Yes! I am on my way to pursuing my dream,* I thought. Things were going according to plan, but then, later that week, I received more news. That tidbit of information changed the trajectory of my life forever, those dreaded words for a teenager to hear; you're pregnant. *How could this happen? What am I going to do...?*

I was so confused, but I knew I had to make a decision between going to college or having a baby.

I know! I will abort the pregnancy and no one will ever know, that way I can go to college in the fall. I was not going to let anything come between me and my future. I did not tell the baby's father – I reasoned with myself, there was no need to tell him anything. I was not keeping the baby. We only had sex one time after his prom, we weren't in a serious relationship and I was sure it would not matter to him either way. Besides that, I had decided I did not want any children. I hated being around little winey kids. I know hate is a strong word, but I really did not like being around kids.

My abortion plans were disrupted because somehow, my mother found out. She mandated that I have the baby and as my punishment she refused to pay for my college. Reluctantly, I ended up telling the baby's father I was pregnant. A lot of good it did – I essentially went through the pregnancy alone. He was no help whatsoever. He had no job, no car, and no future. I was not excited about becoming a mother but because I knew I had to take care of me and my baby, I enrolled in a business school to learn some office skills to help secure a decent job. My dream of being a neurosurgeon shattered and drifted away in the wind. That was the beginning of many years of bad decisions, bad relationships, and as a result I hid from the world.

Mask # 2

The second mask I put on was to cover my shame and feelings of being a failure. At the age of 18, I gave birth to a healthy baby boy. I was young, naïve and inexperienced at life, and least expected to have a baby at such an early age. In high school, I was always quiet, shy, and kept to myself. I knew the popular kids because I shared classes with them, but I never hung out with them. I was an A-B Honor roll student and my classes were advanced courses. I guess you could say, I was academically inclined but did not know much about the streets. You see, my mother sheltered me. I did not know what the ghetto, welfare, or food stamps were until I was in my twenties.

Although I was quiet in school, I was not a pushover – I just chose to keep to myself. The relationship with my son's father was extremely toxic. We attempted to make it work for the sake of the baby, but he became violent and *tried* to beat me. I emphasize the word tried because I fought back. I could not grasp the concept of a man or anyone else for that matter, hitting on me, while standing there taking the abuse. Whenever he would try to lay a hand on me, I would fight back. We finally parted ways when my son was about six months old. I can't even say I was upset about it either, because I did not love him. I remember being adamant about not marrying him when my mother tried to force me to marry him because she thought it was the right thing to do. I flat out refused. I was too young to get married anyway, I was only 18! I had to embrace my life as a new mother but it did not make sense to me to make a bad situation worse by adding the title wife to the situation. Truthfully, I do not think I ever loved him, but after we broke-up, something changed in me.

Having my son forced me to grow up quickly. I was a single mother working three jobs hoping I could provide for me and my baby. Ironically, I have never been on any government assistance even after becoming a single mother. God was truly looking after me and my son. He had a plan for my life, but I just did not know it then. After that relationship ended, I started on a downward spiral of bad relationships. I allowed myself to be used by men for my body and this went on for the majority of my early adult life. As a result, I gave myself to a great number of men. Most of the men I was involved with were much older than I was. Later in life, I realized I was seeking a father figure in older men, longing for someone to love and take care of me as a father would. I am not telling you this to make excuses, it is quite the opposite, I am telling you this because, one; I promised you I would be transparent and two; as you read this book you are going to see how all these things I went through as bad as they seem were for a greater purpose.

Mask # 3

Dating older men was a big mistake. I dated an older guy for about two years who was mentally abusive, although he never hit me or was physically abusive, he broke me emotionally. I remember going out with my friends one night and he decided he would punish me for going out. My friends and I loved to party and have a good time and we would always close the nightclubs down and would party until the lights were turned on. That night I drove my car, and when we walked out of the club to the parking lot, my car was nowhere to be found. We stood there in the parking spot where I had parked the car and all of a sudden one of my friends yelled, "Sandra, there is...!" as he was leaving the parking lot. Unbeknown to me, he had a set of keys to my car. I caught him just before he turned on the feeder road and asked him where my car was. He had moved my car over to some office buildings on the other side of the club because he was upset that I was hanging with my friends.

That was one of many mind games he played. The last straw for me was when his cousin, who was a stylist came over to style my hair. They were laughing and talking and I chimed into the conversation. Obviously he did not like what I said, so while his cousin had a hot marcel iron in my head and one on the burner, he got a fork, stuck the prongs into my neck and threatened to stab me if I ever disrespected him again. I was quiet for the rest of the day. The next day, I called him and told him he needed to come home, because I thought someone was breaking into the apartment. When he opened the door, I was sitting on the couch positioned so he could see me pointing a loaded 12-gauge shotgun at him. I told him if he ever threatened to kill me again or put his hands on me, I would kill him and was willing to serve time in the penitentiary for doing so. Two days later he moved out of the apartment while I was at work taking all my furniture, leaving me one plate, one fork and one glass. He filled the washer with water and placed all of my dry clean only garments in it. I failed to mention, he moved in with me and everything in that apartment I had purchased. Needless to say, we broke up and I put on another mask. This one covered my low self-esteem and desperation, I wanted to be loved.

After that relationship, I stopped trusting men and decided, I was not going to be tied down with just one relationship, I was going to have some fun. I decided to sleep with men "for sport". I told myself if men could do it, I could do it too. This was my way of protecting myself from being hurt by men (or so I thought). No more abuse, no more lies, no more heartbreak. No harm, no foul, right? Everybody got what they wanted – it was a win-win situation. Little did I know, every time I gave myself sexually to a man, I was tainting my temple and giving my pearls to swine.

I had given myself to Christ as a teenager, Jesus lived within me, but he could not dwell in an unholy temple. To protect myself from contracting any sexually transmitted diseases, I collected condoms and made a tree out of them sitting it next to my bed (had to protect myself). The irony is I was protecting my physical body but not my spiritual being, and I soon found out, God was not pleased with my lifestyle.

Mask # 4

One night, I was invited to a house party and one of my friends came along with me. When we arrived, I ran into a guy I knew from high school. I secretly had a crush on him back then. We flirted around with each other and kept the conversations going after the party. He was cool, I saw him as more of a friend than a love interest or conquest. We had a connection, he was easy to talk to and he made me laugh, he was a good buddy. We would hang-out and shoot the breeze, but it was strictly platonic, until one night he asked me,

'Why aren't you trying to come on to me?'

I responded to him, 'Because I do not see you that way, I really like you as a friend.'

He expressed his interest in me and we started dating. Our relationship was great. But I had another life that he knew nothing about. I was still "having fun" with other guys. Yes, I was trapped in fornication and promiscuity. The enemy can make sin look so extravagant and enjoyable. We were growing closer and closer and I started developing intimate feelings for him, I fell in love. I know it sounds weird, but it came out of nowhere. Love slapped me in the face and I started seeing myself as his wife. I let my guard down and boom, it happened. He told me he and his wife decided to work their marriage out. *Wife!? How long have you been married?* So many questions ran through my head, *how could I not know that he was married?* We broke-up, but not for long. I picked up another mask. This mask covered up my feeling of looking like a fool and homewrecker.

Even in your sin, God sees you!

Mask # 5

About three months later he decided to divorce his wife because he said his heart was with me. We decided to get back together, but I had turned back to my old ways of using men for my amusement while he was trying to reconcile with his wife. But there was something different about him, he was all in. He treated me like a queen! He catered to me. I just knew we were going to get married. I attended all of the family functions, birthdays, and holiday celebrations. We had been dating for two years, and then out of the blue, he called me and told me we needed to break-up – just like that, with no explanation. We were not having any disagreements or problems in our relationship. I had noticed he was a little distant, but because he could be moody at times, I thought nothing of it. I was devastated. Two weeks later, I received a call from a mutual acquaintance of ours. During that phone call, I found out he had a baby on the way with someone else and did not know how to tell me. That was it for me! I decided not to get involved in a serious relationship with any man and I put on yet another mask. This mask covered up my bitterness and anger towards men. God was intervening and moving on my behalf. Little did I know, the heartache I experienced was getting ready to push me closer to Jesus! It is interesting how a negative experience can transform into being the pivotal turning point in your life.

After the break-up, a shift happened within me. I could not explain it, but I no longer found it fun to sleep with a lot of different men, but I could not stop myself from doing it. Every time, I would spend the night with a man, I would feel spiritually drained the next day, but I kept doing it, I could not stop. I was addicted to sex. Each time I slept with them, I left behind a piece of me. There was a spiritual war going on within me.

One day, my best friend invited me to her church musical. As far back as I can remember, I have loved musicals, so I agreed to meet her there. She stood me up but since I was already there, I decided to stay and enjoy the choir music by myself. There was only one seat left and it was on the front pew. I took my seat and listened to the different choirs sing. I remember the choir started to sing their rendition of the Mississippi Mass Choir's song, "Your Grace and Mercy," , *"Your grace and mercy brought me through, I am living this moment because of you, I want to thank you and praise you too. Your grace and mercy brought me through."* When the lead singer sung the words, *"Thank You for saving a sinner like me, to tell the world salvation is free,"* tears started flowing like a river down my face. I sat on the front row of the pew, just crying and praying telling the Lord I was tired of living the way I was living, and I was not going to ask forgiveness because I knew I was not going to stop. Spiritually, I was a mess and God needed to clean me up for the divine assignment he had for me. One thing is for sure, I knew I could not continue down the path I was on. I knew I needed to stop having premarital sex, but I did not have the will power to stop. I asked God to send me a husband so that I would not have to fornicate anymore. Even in that place, The Holy Spirit saw through my mask of portraying to be happy in my life of fornication and promiscuity. Even in sin, God saw me!

It was not long after my encounter with God that I stopped committing fornication, but I still kept to my commitment of not getting into a serious relationship with a man. I had settled quite well in my life of not dating.

One day my son was in the restroom talking, or so we thought. My sister asked him who he was talking to, he replied,

'I am not talking, I am praying.'

'What are you praying for?' my sister asked.

'I asked God to send me a daddy," he replied.

I thought nothing of the prayer, but my sister told me God was going to answer him because he hears the prayers of children. I never thought my decision to go through life without a companion would have a negative impact on my son. His father was not active in his life when we parted ways; and we never spoke to each other again until the time he promised my son he would visit him. I remember that day vividly, it was like a scene from a movie. Excited about seeing his father, my son got dressed, grabbed his basketball and sat on it in the driveway. He sat there for hours only coming in the house to get a drink of water and to use the bathroom. Just as the sun was going down, he looked at me with tears in his eyes and asked me if I thought his daddy had forgotten him. Later that night, while at work, I called his father to find out what happened. He decided he had better things to do that to see his son. I told him he would never put my son through that again and that I was going to file child support on him and he response was, "I do not care, file it, I will go to jail before I give you a dime. Anyways, there I will get three hots (meals) and a cot (bed)." I knew I was dealing with a fool, so I cursed him out and hung up. I did not file child support on him. I reasoned that, doing so would give him rights to see our son and subject him to days like he experienced earlier that day. I decided take care of my son myself without him. I never heard from his father again. That added to the layer of bitterness and discontentment I already felt towards men.

Within a year after my heart was broken, I started to build up my inner strength again. I could finally listen to a Toni Braxton CD without breaking down in tears at the red lights while driving. A very good friend of mine invited me out with her and her boyfriend, I of course declined. She was not accepting no for an answer. She told me it was time for me to get out and mingle again, but I was not hearing that, I had sworn off men. I was done! She ignored me and dragged me to a night club with her and her date. While she and her date were out on the dance floor, a guy named Kelvin walked up and started a conversation with me. We ended up dancing and having a great time. We exchanged numbers but I was not the least bit interested in him. He seemed nice but in the back of my mind, I kept hearing the words, *he cannot be trusted*. So, I did not give him the time of day. We would meet for happy hour, but it was nothing serious. He consistently asked if he could come over for a visit during the week and just talk. I let him stop by from time to time to see me. When he would stop by, he always made it a point to play video games with my son. After about a month or so, he asked me out on a formal date, dinner and a movie. We watched the movie, "Waiting to Exhale" and afterwards went to Pappasito's Mexican restaurant.

The next day was our second date and we went to church together. Things were going well and moving fast, this felt real to me. He started to renew my trust in men again and we became exclusive, but I was still reserved and guarded. It seemed as if the prayer my son prayed just a few months prior was being answered. As we grew deeper in the relationship, he received a job offer in another state and he asked me to come with him. I declined, stating, I could not follow him as LaSandra Wells but I can go as LaSandra Collins. A week later he proposed, and I accepted. Kelvin decided not to accept the job in Atlanta but he still wanted to get married. We elected not to have a wedding, instead, Kelvin bought me a nice ring and furnished our first apartment. A month before Kelvin and I got married, we found a church home. He got up and took me by the hand and we joined together as a couple.

We married five months and two days after we met. Kelvin and I exchanged vows in front of the fireplace in the apartment we were renting. I realized God separated me from the man I thought would be my husband to make room in my heart for the husband he had picked out for me. Even when we can't see God working and it feels like nothing is happening, we must trust His plan and the process. God had not revealed his entire plan for me yet and my marriage was just the beginning of the plans He had for me.

I entered my marriage with a lot of baggage, wearing many masks and it was not long before Kelvin and I had major issues within our marriage. I was lost and unhappy. My luggage was so full that the clasps eventually gave way and my dirty laundry spilled over into our relationship forcing me to face those painful experiences that caused me to wear the masks for years. I had not healed mentally or spiritually. Each painful life experience took me back to the five years old girl who experienced trauma with the murder of her father. Of course, I did not fully understand at the time what was going on nor did I understand the grieving process and how it had shaped my life. I was a functioning, dysfunctional person, meaning I only existed and was not living.

After ten years of unhappy marital bliss, in 2006, I decided to separate from my husband leaving my house and our toddler son, and moved into an apartment. My oldest son had already left for college. Besides the loss of my father, and two miscarriages, me walking away from my marriage was the most devastating and traumatic experience in my life!

The first week in that apartment alone, I asked myself the burning question, most ask themselves after making a promise not to do something again. *"How did I get back here?"* I promised myself, I was not going to do that again. But I did not have any answers, all I had were questions, and what felt like a bunch of regrets. I was in a bad place and had no idea how I was going to recover from the blow that life had given me.

Has someone ever held an intervention with you? The type of intervention where they point out the path that you are on and show you how it is going to lead to your self-destruction if you do not change? Well, that is what happened to me in my apartment. I could no longer run or hide from who God was calling me to be. I had to stop living the lifestyle I was living. It was getting me nowhere fast and preventing me from answering the call God had on my life. Can you relate to any part of my story? Whether your story is similar to mine or totally different, it doesn't matter. If you are living beneath your privilege or outside of the will of God, you need to change. In order to address any problem, you must first recognize there is a problem, then, you can begin to correct and turn away.

I tried to fix myself on my own and I left God out of the process. You should never attempt to fix yourself by leaving out the one who created you to begin with. Take it from me, it cannot be done. That would be like a surgeon performing surgery on himself. It is virtually impossible to do. But there is one who can mend you, if you just let him. Never in a million years would I have imagined being here, doing what I am doing right now, inspiring, and ministering, and encouraging others to be their true and authentic selves in Christ. This just did not happen overnight. My bad experiences affected me to the core and the journey I took to reveal the person God called me to be would be a winding road of poor judgment, which led to poor decisions that ultimately resulted in me being an empty shell of a person, wandering with no sense of spiritual direction or destination.

I mentioned earlier about the encounter I had with God at the church musical. That was my first intervention by the Holy Spirit. He prompted me to ask myself the questions below. I started by asking myself with the following questions:

1. Girl, you know you got to get yourself together, right?

2. Aren't you tired of living like this?

3. Do you honestly believe you can keep living like this and reach your full potential?

4. How will remaining in this lifestyle impact your future?

I want you to meditate on these questions as you take the road to your journey to healing.

THE PAIN OF SIN

Temporary pleasures lead to life full of pain
A glimmer of sunshine hides behind the storms and rain
Decision to please self leads to hell and frustration
None of which were factored in my equation.

I sit and I ponder, *what shall I do next?*
For I have strayed from Jesus and my soul is vexed.
I pace back and forth within the corners of my mind
The peace I am seeking I simply cannot find.

The decision to please self is truly my plight
Because I have left Christ out of my life
As my flesh and spiritual beings continue to fight
I can hear Jesus gently whisper, "I am the Light."

While I struggle to cut loose this life in the fast lane
I am reminded of all my actions and feel so ashamed
But Jesus says to me, "There is no need to have fear
When you accept me your slate is wiped clear"

I repented and gave Jesus His rightful place in my heart

He is now head of my life, where He should have been from the start

He leads and I surely follow, He's my *"strength for today and bright hope for tomorrow."*

CHAPTER TWO
MY METAMORPHOSIS

Metamorphosis:

"The transformation from a spiritually immature person into a completely different one, by divine intervention." LaSandra Collins

By now you are probably wondering, what happened in my marriage that caused me to leave my child and husband behind. To be honest, I had the same question. At the time I was broken, empty, confused, fragile, and I had reached my breaking point. I was wearing so many masks, I did not recognize myself. I felt like a stranger in my home as I failed at attempts to hide years of hurt and pain. With all the masks I piled on coupled with the emotional baggage – I never addressed, I hit a brick wall and as a result, I was emotionally and spiritually destitute with no identity.

Mask # 6

During the early years of my marriage, I had picked up another mask. I was hiding loneliness and unhappiness. I could not continue in the spiritual state I was in, so I took an inventory of my life. I wanted to understand how and why I was in such a desolate state of being. I thought I had a good relationship with God because I had accepted him into my heart as a teenager. I did the right things like praying often and attending church every Sunday. I was a faithful and loving wife, and a good mother to my sons. But yet I still wondered, *What is happening to me? Why am I so unhappy? Who am I? and Why is my marriage failing?* Those were the questions, that I soon found the answers too. I had to do some soul searching but it was not until my second encounter with God that the answers were revealed.

During the course of me seeking answers, I picked up my love for writing again. I wrote quite often as a teenager; it gave me so much joy. When I started writing this time, I wrote little devotionals to comfort myself from the pain I was feeling. Each day, I would find a scripture and write it out on paper to minister to myself. Writing came easy to me; I wrote poems and short stories while in high school. When Kelvin and I would have a disagreement, I would write a poem or something spiritually inspirational to help me cope with what was going on. I kept writing using tablets and pens everywhere so when I had inspiration to write, I could easily grab them and write. Writing was my escape and it gave me peace.

My husband was the primary breadwinner in our household, so when I moved out, I had to maintain my own household by working a full-time job and a part-time job while remaining a full-time student in graduate school. To say the least, my plate was full, and I was under a lot of stress. I suffered from insomnia because of the stress. I remember one night I cried all night and could not sleep. I got out of bed, went to my living room and fell on my knees and prayed. I wept as I prayed and stayed on my knees for what seemed like an hour or so. Before I ended my prayer, I heard the voice of

Jesus say, "You made your husband, your God and I created you for my purpose not his!" I ended my prayer and began to ponder what God had revealed to me. I took a trip down memory lane to take inventory of my life and the behaviors that led to me unknowingly making Kelvin my God in the place of Jesus. In essence, God was showing me I worshipped Kelvin because though at the time he was a lousy husband he was a great father and provider. He did all the things a father would do; he took great care of me as a father would. This was something I never experienced as a child because my father was taken from us during my formative years. Daughters need their fathers. A father-daughter relationship sets the example of how she interacts with men as an adult. It was then that I began to discover that my issues stemmed from me not having my father around as a child, but this was just a tip of the iceberg. I had to make some changes and put my husband in his rightful place. God didn't want me to love Kelvin any less, He wanted me to properly prioritize the marriage. Above anything else, my relationship with Christ was my lifeline and anything else – no matter how important, should have never come before that.

During this self-evaluation, I discovered that the emotional imbalances and insecurities had started with the death of my father. That negative experience was the root cause of all the masks I had put on over the years. After my discovery, I started cleaning out my closet spiritually. I knew I needed God's guidance to face my past and unravel the mysteries of what brought me to where I was at that moment. My prayer stuck with me and I kept what God had whispered in the back of my mind. I needed to reconcile some personal skeletons before addressing my marriage. I started unpacking my life one by one, purging those things that did not fit. I began the process of shedding the layers I had put on over the years, so that I could see what was underneath. I did a lot of purging; that is, taking out the trash and releasing past hurts so that I could move forward with my life. Before I could address my marital problem, I had to address the root of my problems. I had to take the responsibility to address my issues and not focus on the faults of my husband.

Removing the Masks

I started from the beginning, the night my innocence was stolen. I had to forgive that teenager for violating me. It was tough, because he truly stole something from me, I could never get back. Even now as I write this story, it saddens me. I can't harp on it, because it held me hostage for too many years already and I had to let it go. I had to forgive him if I was ever going to be in position for what God had for me. I realized that we were teenagers, making immature choices. I am not excusing what he did, but it is likely that he did not understand he was breaking the law with this act or that he was taking my innocence. I had to release that horrible experience for my own sanity and healing. Rape is never the victim's fault. My fault in that situation was not feeling my relationship was strong enough with my mother to call her. In hindsight, I know she would have dropped everything to come get me. But if you can imagine as a 16-year-old kid, who was terrified of her mother, I did not have that foresight. I could only think that she was going to kill me and I was going to die a slow death if I missed curfew. That day I discarded the mask of embarrassment.

Next, I reflected on my first male relationship. I pondered what I needed to learn from that experience. I had harbored a lot of resentment towards him, for not helping me with the rearing or financially with our son and for physically abusing me. It was certainly time to let go of what transpired between us, he was long gone. He died while paying his debt to society when my son was 13-year-old. I forgave him. Once I forgave him, I had to forgive myself. I admitted at how disappointed I had been with my life because I became pregnant and could not fulfill my childhood dream of being a neurosurgeon. One of the most valuable lessons I learned that I share with my children and others, is to be careful the mate you create children with. Everyone is not meant to be a permanent fixture in your life. One beautiful thing did come out of that relationship and that is my son. I love him with all my heart. That day I removed the mask of feeling like a failure.

The next mask I took off was the mask of shame. This one took some time and was tied to my promiscuity and the decision to date older men. When I was honest and realized I was trying to replace the void of my father, I made peace with the fact that I could never replace my father's love for me with multiple lovers. It was impossible to do. We cannot replace people with other people, although we often try. The other reason and a critical fact is a father is not meant to be a lover, he is meant to be a protector and a provider. That privilege is set aside for the person that is meant to be your spouse. Shedding the mask of shame was tied to several masks I needed to take off, but before I could do that I needed to forgive the older guy who broke me emotionally and caused me tremendous mental anguish. I needed to face that relationship and this time I had to reopen some scars and cut out the infection. I held a grudge against him for the years he tormented me day-in and day-out for over two years. I suffered a miscarriage, as a result of the stress he subjected me to – mentally, he destroyed me. I let go of the hurt he inflicted upon me and broke the mask of desperation. It was a little while later that I was able to break the mask of low self-esteem.

They say you never truly get over your first love, and that person will always have a place in your heart. The mask to conceal my bitterness and anger, would not be easily broken. This one was often exhibited in my personality and my interactions with Kelvin or any other man. The truth is I had no respect for men, because of all the things they had done to me to over the years. That revelation was also the beginning of me peeling back the onion of what went wrong in my marriage, but we will discuss that later. My first love was also my confidant, while I was separated from my husband. You might ask why? Well, we were really good friends before we started dating all those years ago and I could talk to him about anything. He was one of the only people I knew that I could be myself around. We were strictly friends, and nothing more. I still honored my wedding vows although Kelvin and I were separated. Because he knew me so well, he was instrumental in helping me get rid of that mask. I remember speaking with him one day, and I asked him,

'Why do men cheat?' Before, he could respond, I asked him, 'Why did you cheat on me? What's wrong with me that men always cheat on me?'

I still had a burning desire to find out the answer to that question although it had been ten years since we had ended our relationship. But truthfully, I never received closure and a part of me needed that. Our relationship ended abruptly, and it left an emotional scar. It took me quite some time to move past what had happened between us. Oddly enough, he answered me. He told me he could not speak for other men, but when we were dating, he was in a bad place mentally. He hated women because of what his ex-wife had done to him. He admitted that he mistreated a lot of women and his regret was not marrying the one he should have married years ago.

He then said, 'I should have married you, and I am sorry for everything that I put you through.'

I accepted his apology and it turned out that was the closure I needed to move past our relationship. Unbeknownst to me, I was still grieving over our relationship, but I did not realize it and my grief had spilled over into my marriage. I burned the mask of bitterness. That was just one layer of the hurt, I was still angry and needed to face the music, it was time I addressed one more man; my husband. Spiritually, I was getting stronger, I could feel some of the weight falling off of me.

After my conversation with my ex, I got down on my knees once again. I remember telling God, I was giving him every facet of my life and I was not taking it back because I was tired. I told him I was going to follow Him, because I knew I could not do it myself. I rededicated myself to Jesus resolving to do whatever it was He wanted me to do. I sought forgiveness for turning my back on Him. The next day, I went to church and after service, I became a new member.

Daily I was writing spiritual inspirations to get me through the day. I would share them with my close colleagues who suggested I should write a book. I would always reject the idea because I was writing to help myself overcome my own situations. After the closure with my ex-boyfriend, I realized that I had been subconsciously pining over the relationship I ended before my marriage. With this finally behind me, I was ready to tackle my marriage. I was in a good place mentally and spiritually. I heard the voice of God again, but this time, He told me I needed to be honest with myself about my role in the marriage. He went on to say, I was not fulfilling my role as a wife, I had made him my God, and I was also mistreating him. Now I know that sounds somewhat contradictory, but it is not, it is no different than us telling God that we love him, yet we go days without talking to him. We put other things before Him, and sometimes we only call him when we are in trouble. God was right, I was very disrespectful to Kelvin. I did not honor him as my husband or the head of the household. I would undermine all his decisions, which was strange because I chose to marry him so why would I not trust him to lead? The past hurts supported these actions. That was the baggage I brought into the relationship and marriage. I had never healed. I jumped from relationship to relationship always finding a new person to date to conceal the pain. I never took the time to be alone. Not only was I still nursing a wound of my past relationship, I was bitter towards Kelvin, holding him hostage and making him suffer for all the things other men did to hurt me. I know, that was terrible, that old adage reigned true, "Hurt people, hurt people." But in the end, I hurt myself, Kelvin, and our children too, because I found myself separated, facing divorce, which was something I never wanted.

Do you know that sometimes the decisions you make and the things you do, not only affect you, they can also impact at least one other person? In this case, my decisions inflicted pain on Kelvin and our children. It is difficult to console others when you are hurting yourself, I had just enough strength to keep myself going but I did not have enough to pour into anyone else. After my new-found discovery, my sister and I visited a church I had been wanting to check out. The praise leader was awesome! She started singing, "Your latter will be greater." The spirit was really moving during this service. I was worshipping God, when the Holy Spirit came upon me. I started dancing in the spirit, and all of a sudden, I was alone with God. It was just me and Jesus! He told me everything was going to be alright with me and my marriage and that I would be blessed. It seemed in that moment as if I had spent a lifetime with Jesus but in reality it was only a few minutes. I had never felt freer in my life than at that moment when God spoke to me. From that day forward, daily I welcomed the Holy Spirit to guide me. I truly learned to lean on, depend, and trust God. It was not easy at first for me to let go of controlling my life, I would give my concerns to God, but then I would take them back because it seemed as if nothing was happening. In my mind, God was not moving fast enough, but I had to learn, He moves in his timing and not mine. He used my marriage to teach me this lesson.

Have you ever felt like you were living in a nightmare that would never end? Well, this is how I felt every morning when I woke up in that apartment alone. It took me months to dissect where I went wrong in my marriage, but I was not ready to talk to Kelvin, we were still on bad terms. That first year of separation, we constantly bickered and argued. I later found out that God was dealing with him about his part in our failed marriage. Deep down inside, I always knew God picked my husband for me, but like many I took matters into my own hands leaving God out of the decision-making process. Have you ever taken matters into your own hand, even though you knew what you were about to do was not in the will of God? Well, I had had it with being separated, and living in isolation; there was a third party lingering around, Kelvin and I figured, I would write myself out the equation. I filed for a divorce. In my spirit, I knew I should not have because it didn't feel right but being a strong and stubborn woman, I did it anyways. Three days later, Kelvin came to my job and I told him I had filed for a divorce. I never in a million years would have expected the reaction I witnessed! With tears in his eyes,

Kelvin asked me why, I filed for a divorce, shocked, at his response and the tears welling in his eyes, I told him I thought I was giving him what he wanted, to be free. I was truly taken aback by Kelvin's response, but I knew I needed to put it out my head. I had class that evening, and I was not my usual self. Up until then I had done a pretty good job of not letting my personal life spill over into my education, but Kelvin's reaction really shook me, I felt like I had been gut punched. My professor noticed I was not myself and he asked me what was wrong, there was a rush of pinned up tears that started falling from my eyes. He stopped the class and prayed for me. I felt better after that prayer but in the days to come, I was torn. I knew I was going outside of God's will by filing for the divorce.

Thanksgiving and Christmas had come and gone and I did not spend either holiday with Kelvin, I spent them with my family. Since I could remember, Kelvin and I would always spend New Year's Eve together attending watch night service at church. On December 31, 2007, I went to watch night service alone. I found a seat and sat there in anticipation of hearing the choir sing and a message from God. While sitting there I looked up and there was Kelvin walking towards me. He took the vacant seat next to me and we brought the last night of that year in standing next each other. Kelvin and I were in a place where we could finally communicate without arguing and yelling at one another, but soon we would be opposite of one another in court finalizing our divorce.

The court date to finalize the divorce was in February. The night before our court date, Kelvin called me. He was in London working and he begged me not to show up for court. I told him I was tired; it was best we part ways. I had lost all hope in our marriage, my soul was weary, and I wanted to be free. We stayed on the phone until past midnight, as he tried to convince me not to go through with the divorce. I will never forget what he told me right before we ended that call, 'Sandra, God told me to get my family back together,' his voice trembled while he was saying it. I told him I would think about it, but I still felt like the marriage was over. When I hung up the phone, the spirit of conviction came back again. The Holy Spirit reminded me once more, that I was not doing the right thing. I ignored the prompting and went to sleep.

The next morning, I got up and got dressed but I still did not know what I was going to do. I put on a suit, I wrestled with myself with whether I should go to work or to court. I reasoned that whatever I decided I would be dressed appropriately for either. When I got in my car, I said to myself, wherever the Lord leads me, that is where I am going this morning. The Lord led me to work, I did not go to court. It just did not feel right. I knew, I was not supposed to get a divorce. I spoke to Kelvin that evening, I told him I did not go through with it. We had a long talk, what we discovered was that we still loved each other, but we did not like each other, so year two of our separation, we started dating each other again. We became really acquainted with each other. We were married only five months and two days after we met which is hardly enough time for anyone to get to know one another. It felt good to start dating again. Kelvin would pick me up and take me out every Friday night. We would go to church every Sunday as a family unit. We were committed to working on our marriage. However, there was still an area that he needed to address. The other woman, the third party, was lurking around Kelvin and she was not pleased with our reconciliation. She would call me playing childish games, asking to speak to him or calling to hear what type of background I was in to determine if I was with Kelvin. This went on for months. The last straw was the day she showed up to our place of worship one Sunday morning demanding to speak with Kelvin. She walked up and declared she was going to worship with us that morning. I had done my research and knew she was married, I asked her if her husband would be joining us, she responded, 'no'. Kelvin asked her what she was doing there, she said she needed to speak with him. He asked me to take our young son to his Sunday School class and meet him where we would normally sit in service. As I was escorting my son inside the sanctuary, he looked back and asked me, 'Mommy, why is that lady hitting Daddy?' By the time I looked back, the off-duty police officer was detaining her, I kept walking my son to his class. Kelvin met me as he promised, took my hand and told me everything was okay, the officers arrested her for assault.

In June 2008, Kelvin and I reunited back under the same roof with our son. Before I could move back with him, I had to forgive both myself and him. I had a candid conversation with him about what I had learned while we were apart. I asked him for his forgiveness, and I put the rest in God's hands. But I would soon learn, I still had not fully removed the mask of low self-esteem. Now, I am not saying any of this was easy to do but it was necessary for me to move forward with my life. You may wonder why I went back to him? Well, I knew God put us together and the enemy knew that God put us together too. This meant he was going to use any means necessary to destroy what God created. Matthew 19:6 says, "So they are no longer two, but one flesh. Therefore, what God has joined together, let no one separate." This meant neither Kelvin nor I could tear the marriage apart either.

Looking back on that experience, I know that God isolated me for a little while to get my attention. During that time, He dealt with me as an individual and then as a wife. Through this process, I learned a lot about myself and the sovereignty of God. There is nothing like getting clarity and that experience certainly gave me that. For years, I had been tortured by things I had left unaddressed and unresolved, which almost cost me my marriage and my sanity. But it would not be long before God would reveal how those experiences would serve His purpose for me. Throughout each scenario, I could see God was in control and at work in my life.

Doing the Work

If I was ever going to understand how I got to that place, I needed to start from the beginning. I prayed and did an introspection exploring why I put the mask on to begin with. Though my separating from Kelvin was difficult to do, it was necessary for God to get my attention. He desired a relationship with me, which required me to repent and transform. It took me a while to peel back the layers and discover that a huge part of the issues that occurred with me were unresolved issues stemming from my childhood. I sat up many nights and having conversations with God seeking answers. The more I sought God the more I learned about Him and realized He had His hands on me through it all. As I went through this process, I discovered that my brokenness had a purpose in God's Kingdom.

Now that I have given you some back history about me and the many masks I wore, I want you to take your own assessment. We are going to explore the process I went through to free myself of the masks and embrace this beautiful being that was underneath. Before we move on, I want you to be honest with yourself and answer the following questions:

1. Are you tired of wearing a mask(s)?

2. Do you want to take your mask off?

3. How can you move forward?

4. Is change necessary for you to release your past?

5. What role did you play in my mess?

6. How have your experiences impacted you?

7. How can you be free of past hurts and pain?

I want you to write these questions down and answer them, later we are going to address them. Being truthful with yourself is the only way to healing. You must face and accept the truth regardless of how unattractive it may be. As you can see, none of my story is glamourous and I am not proud of it either, but I needed to find peace and the only way to do it was admitting the truth regardless of how unappealing it was. You must do the same thing. We all have things and experiences in our past that we are not happy about or don't want anyone to know. However, in order for you to heal and truly be released from all the hurt and pain these experiences brought you, you must be honest with yourself.

CHAPTER THREE
HE CALLED ME WORTHY

Now that we have gone through the process of psychoanalyzing me, we are going to move along to the steps I took to remove the many masks I wore for years. I encourage you to take these steps as well to remove your mask and embrace who you are underneath. As you can see, I am nowhere near perfect, I am quite the contrary and some would have judged me and considered me a harlot back then, to put it nicely.

After I took ownership and held myself accountable of my old lifestyle, my behavior and actions towards Kelvin and my blatant omission of God's commandments, I sought forgiveness. Even still I could not shake the feeling that I was worthless to God because I saw myself as damaged good, unworthy of being in his presence. I mean, how could God ever see me as worthy? The things that I had done were shameful, I defied my temple, giving myself to those who were undeserving of me. I was not a perfect wife and on top of all of that, God told me I worshipped Kelvin rather than him. In one of my many conversations with God, I asked him a critical question, "Do you see me as worthy?" I could not grasp the concept that He could ever see me as worthy. *Why would He?* I asked myself, *Look at all you have done?* There were times I felt I had taken a bath in shame and unworthiness, but I realized seeing yourself as unworthy is exactly what the enemy wants you to do. As long as you see yourself as unworthy and undeserving, the more difficult you will find it to see yourself through the eyes of Christ.

Did you know, one of the biggest reasons why we put on

masks is the fear of not being accepted? What if I told you, you do not have to fear being accepted anymore because God loves and accepts you just the way you are? Would you believe me? Well, guess what? You are God's masterpiece! This means God sees you as worthy. I had to start seeing myself as Christ saw me and so do you have to see yourself as Christ sees you.

> *"When we lose our identity, we open the door to self-doubt, the feeling of being unworthy and lack of confidence."*

Oftentimes, we allow things that happened to us and negative experiences to cause us to question our worth and value. When we doubt our value and worth, we are saying God created us imperfect. It is a trick of the enemy to doubt your worth and value. Worthless is not an adjective that God uses to describe you! Quite the contrary, His word says in Psalms 139:14 that you are "Fearfully and wonderfully made." But can we see ourselves the way God sees us?

The first step to seeing yourself as God sees you is getting to know your Creator. God created man and woman in His image. Genesis 1:26 and 31 tells us, "Then God sees everything that He had made, and indeed it was very good." That means you too are God's creation and He sees you as good.

Spending time with God, communicating with Him, and studying His word is the best way to get to know God, His nature and how He sees you. We see in Genesis that God created us in His image and declares it was very good! This is your first indication that God sees you as worthy. Even today, I still spend quality time with God. I enjoy our time together. I had to develop an intimate relationship with Him if I was ever going to understand why He saw me as worthy. As you spend time with God, He will reveal to you who He is and who you are to Him. This is the beginning of you developing your self-identity in Christ.

Identity is critical to building your self-esteem. Lack of identity contributes to lack of self-worth and poor self-esteem, both of which have no place in our hearts and minds. Thoughts like this cause us to be derailed from what God has for us. In a sense, I struggled with my identity. I did not know how to have a relationship with a man, because I never saw that growing up. Understanding your identity in Christ is crucial to seeing yourself as worthy and it contributes to having confidence in who you are (self-esteem). Allow me to reiterate, when we lose our identity, we open the door to self-doubt, the feeling of being unworthy and lack of confidence.

It was not until I realized my identity in Christ that I was able to start peeling off the mask that covered my low self-esteem. This just did not happen overnight, oh no, this mask wanted to stay. It was my security blanket. If I left it on, no one would know deep down inside that I was afraid to be me. I was afraid of rejection, and I was afraid of being seen as a failure, the list went on and on. I had a lot of hang-ups, but when I came to realize I was someone in Christ, all my fears dissipated. Not only did I accept myself in Him, I started to love me as well.

Self-love! Wow, now that is a word I had to get used to saying. Why? Because the lifestyle that I lived was far from me loving myself. But the day I learned who I was in Christ and that He loved me, I also realized I had to start loving myself and so do you. When you love yourself, you will begin to ensure that you do things in the best interest of your well-being, to protect you. Now what does that mean? It means, you stop self-sabotaging yourself and you do those things that preserve your self-esteem and your self-worth. For example, honoring my temple before I got married, would have been practicing self-love and not settling for less than I deserved in a mate. It is not selfish to love yourself, as a matter of fact it is encouraged. Not to worry, learning to love yourself is a process, as I said, it did not happen overnight for me either. As a matter-of-fact it took me years to totally love myself. But as I spent more and more time with God, the revelation of who He is and who I am in Christ made it impossible for me not to love the person I was transforming into. It was Ethel Waters who said, "I am somebody because God don't make no junk." She was right and you should believe you are someone in Christ because everything He created is good.

I learned many things during this process and forgiving myself was by far the toughest thing I had to do. One because when I thought about all the things I suffered and the people who wronged me, I was not on the list. You never really think about the negative impact of the decisions you make and how you hurt yourself all in the vain of having fun. And two, how does one hold herself accountable for the pain she inflicted on herself? I had to school myself on how to forgive myself. Unforgiveness, is the biggest enemy to you being healed and delivered from those people who caused you pain and the pain you caused yourself. When we withhold forgiveness from others, we open the door to such things as bitterness and hatred. We also allow a wedge to separate us from Christ. Forgiveness is essential so that you can move past those experiences that brought you discomfort be it by you or by others. One thing is for sure, refusing to forgive holds you in bondage. I remember, before meeting my husband, I only went to work, and back home, my friends would invite me to different outings but I would tell them it was not safe to come outside. In my mind, it was not safe because I feared people (men) would hurt me. Now, I was not speaking from a physical standpoint, I was speaking from an emotional point-of-view. I was closing myself off from ever meeting anyone because of all the hurt I had suffered in past relationships. But, in order to move on with our life, we have to let go of those bad experiences and forgive those who hurt us. I know what you are thinking, *but you do not know what he did to me… Or I can never forgive her because she did…* Listen, in order for you to receive forgiveness from Christ, you must be willing to forgive those who have done you wrong. Doing so allows you to be free from bondage and insecurities. This alleviates you from feeling as if you have to keep on your mask to hide from others who you really are. I am not saying forgiving someone is an easy feat, because I grappled with it too, but I can tell you, when I did forgive those who I felt hurt me, it was as if a burden was lifted off me.

Sometimes before you can take off the mask you have to forgive yourself. That is right, self-forgiveness is necessary. I had to learn to forgive myself and you will have to do the same. This includes forgiving yourself for the bad choices you made. Yes, and here is what I told myself, *I do not think I did anything wrong, I was responding to what they did.* It does not matter how we justify our actions, if we are hurting ourselves in the process, we must acknowledge our wrongdoing, correct the issue if we can, forgive ourselves, and move on. Have you ever done something so far out of character that you could not believe it yourself? Lord knows I have, and I had to forgive myself.

Years ago, I did something I thought I would never do because it was just not in my nature or character. The enemy constantly reminded me of what I did, he would not let me forget it. I remember, calling my best friend, Shaunda about a month after the incident. I told her I could not believe what I had done. I told Shaunda, I asked God for forgiveness, I was sorry for what I had done, and I could not believe I had lost self-control. I was so guilt stricken. As I was talking and wallowing in self-pity, Shaunda said bluntly, 'LaSandra, you have repented, Jesus has forgiven you, now forgive yourself, let it go and move on.' So that is what I am going to tell you. If you have not done so, ask Christ to forgive you, forgive yourself, and move on. Forgiveness is the key to not only relinquishing your mask but it also answers the critical question of, *are you worthy?* Yes, you are because Christ laid down his life for you and through salvation when you seek forgiveness, He so graciously does. When we do not forgive ourselves, we can stifle and unwittingly hold ourselves back from moving forward. Often times the greatest opponent we face is ourselves because we lack the capacity or we are unwilling to forgive.

An intimate relationship with Christ was the beginning of me answering the critical question of whether I was worthy? Though in my mind, I was not worthy, because of all the things I had done. I had to learn to forgive myself and others, love myself and see myself as Christ sees me. This was the only way I could begin to accept that I was worthy and embrace who I am in Christ.

Before we move on, I want you to be honest and answer the questions below:

1. Look in the mirror, do you like what you see?

2. Can you see yourself as Christ sees you?

3. Do you see yourself as being good at anything? (Write down what you are good at.)

4. Do you love yourself?

5. Are you withholding forgiveness from others? If so, why?

6. Can you forgive yourself? Are you willing to forgive those who hurt you?

Now review the questions from the previous chapter. How did those answers influence how you see yourself? Put your answers in a safe place because we will refer to them later.

SET FREE

I'm stuck, stuck, stuck in my own insecurities

I'm stuck, stuck, stuck my fear has imprisoned me

I'm stuck, stuck, stuck in this place and nowhere to go

I'm stuck, stuck, stuck and hide so no one will know.

I pray, I pray, I pray that somehow my pain will end

I pray, I pray, I pray that I will gain the strength to stand

I pray, I pray, I pray that I will see what He sees in me

I pray, I pray, I pray that I can finally be who He called me
to be.

I'm free, I'm free, I'm free greater is He that is in me

I'm free, I'm free, I'm free His Spirit has revived me

I'm free, I'm free, I'm free in Christ I have liberty

I'm free, I'm free, I'm free Christ has given me victory.

CHAPTER FOUR
THERE IS A STRANGER IN THE MIRROR

When you look in the mirror, what do you see? Do you see the person God is calling you to be? Do you even recognize yourself? When was the last time you looked at yourself in the mirror? Not to ensure your makeup was perfect; every strand of hair was in place or your clothes fitted just the way you wanted them to. I mean when was the last time you looked in the mirror in admiration of what you saw beneath the makeup and the clothes? There were days, I did not like what I saw in the mirror, heck, I did not even have mirrors in my home, other than the one that was hanging over the sink in the bathroom. And, when I did look in the mirror, because of all the masks I wore, I did not even recognize the person that was staring back at me.

I mentioned earlier about the day, I fell to my knees and told God I was tired of hitting the brick wall of life. That was my breakthrough, the day I realized I had to take off my many masks and embrace who God called me to be. I remember telling God, I was giving him every facet of my life, from that day forward, I was going to let him lead me and guide me. I surrendered everything to him. Immediately after that prayer, I felt a change taking place on the inside but did not quite understand what was going on. The next day, I woke up early, I got dressed, I drove myself to church. I rededicated my life to Christ, vowing to be everything he called me to be. But I wondered where to start. That following Wednesday, I attended mid-week service and the guest pastor's sermon was titled, "Girl, get yourself together." At the end of the sermon, I had the answer to my question! I looked in the mirror, doing introspection and taking inventory of my life so that I could get myself together. I had to retrace the steps that led me to that point before I could get to how to move forward.

I had strayed as far as God would allow me to, it was now time for me to accept that God created me for a purpose. It was time for me to meet the person, I had done a good job of suppressing for many years. I had to introduce myself to the stranger within, that is, the woman God was calling forward. But in order for me to meet her, I had to confront the ugly truth. It was time to identify and define the masks I had worn for so many years, and finally understanding why I put them on to begin with so that I would not grab them again for comfort.

Let me warn you, this might be an emotional process for you, it may cause you to have to open up some wounds that did not heal properly so that you can cut out the infection that caused you to put the masks on to conceal who you are. Now, as I said this may be painful, because exploring your past especially if it was plagued with bad experiences can be emotionally taxing. It pained me to relive some of the hurts I experienced back then, but if I was going to ever be free, I had to go back down memory lane, take the scab off, reopening the wound so that it could heal properly. Only this time the salve I used to heal was the blood of Jesus and the good news is you can use some too.

> *"When emotional trauma is left unaddressed it will manifest itself in other ways, either you are going to deal with trauma; or the trauma will deal with you."*

As I referenced previously, I knew I had to take off the masks, which meant I had to first identify the masks I was wearing. It was necessary so that I could continue my transformation into the woman I am today. Earlier, I told you I traced all my bad decisions in men to the loss of my father at a very young age. The masks of abandonment and insecurity covered my face for years before I piled on the others. Because I was so young, I really did not go through the grieving process and mourn the loss of my father. I have a saying, when emotional trauma is left unaddressed, it will manifest itself in other ways. Either you are going to deal with trauma, or the trauma will deal with you. The latter is exactly what happened to me, the pain of the loss of my father laid dormant for many years, but it started surfacing in my early adult years. It was not until I separated from my husband that I truly understood the hamster wheel I was on. I did not speak to a therapist, well, not in the sense of a licensed professional anyway. I spoke with Christ, who can be whatever you need. However, speaking with a licensed professional is an option and I encourage you to do so if you feel you need to.

My masks were my deflective and protective shields, I put them on so that others would not see the frail person I was on the inside, that timid person who needed acceptance and love.

I hid behind those masks so that no one could hurt me. Over the years, my bad decisions caused me pain, and at the source of that pain were the actions of men. But in going through this process, I realized, I made myself easy prey for the hunters (men) and my masks were hiding me from myself. Promiscuity opened up the door for these men to devour me. I felt as if I was the target and they were the hunters. I created an arena for their amusement. We know where my masks came from; let me ask you, do you know where your mask came from? Why did you put your mask on?

I discovered during this process that God was calling me to a higher purpose, but I was not quite ready just yet to answer the call. It took me years to pile on all those masks, I needed to take time to reflect, a little more. In retrospect, me putting my many masks on was an attempt to run away and hide from my traumatic experiences. The very thing I was trying to hide from, essentially found me and caused me to distort my identity and separate myself from Christ. I had to re-introduce myself to me.

Have you ever felt as if you did not know who you were, because of some of the things you had done and been through? Well, allow me to help you get re-acquainted with yourself. Like me, you are going to have to identify where your mask came from; how you picked up the mask, and why you still have it on. You are going to have to make a decision to take the mask off and get acquainted with who you are beneath the mask. Underneath my masks, the stranger I saw in the mirror staring back at me was a perseverer, who faces adversity head-on, knowing through Christ she can do anything because she is mighty in the Lord and faithful. Though she has endured many trials, she overcame them all.

Although I knew I was worthy, I still battled with taking

the mask off and leaving them off for good. Now remember, I told you this process was not going to be easy, in fact, sometimes even now thoughts of who am I surface; but the difference now is that I know who I am and whose I am. I am equipped with the spiritual tools I need to slay those thoughts before they are able to manifest in my life.

I never looked at myself in the mirror and when I did, I did not know who the woman staring back at me was. I wore masks and put up facades for so long, I did not recognize myself. I made a conscious decision to surrender. I told God I was His. I was tired, I had tried everything but God, the one who could truly set me free. With Him with me every step of the way, I was able confront my past, uncover why I put those masks on, and truly heal. It took me almost two years to discover that perseverance was a part of my DNA, and even then from time-to-time I wrestled with not putting the mask back on. I had to constantly remind myself that I was everything Christ said I was. After some time, I started to fully embrace the woman I was called to be.

Before we move on, take a moment to ponder the questions I asked you earlier, they were the foundational questions to help you identify the root cause of when and why you put your mask on to begin with. As you uncover your root cause you will gradually see yourself differently, you will see the person you were before the mask. Now, this can be tricky, because the person you were before the mask may not necessarily be the person God is calling you to be. I encourage you to seek God in this process and allow Him to introduce you to the woman in the mirror. The person He has known was there all alone. It is time you get to know her as well.

Denying Self

Today, I will deny self the privilege of hindering my success.

I will not let self-pride prevent me from asking for help when I need to be guided.

I will not let self-doubt stifle my dreams or self-pity prevent me from moving forward.

I will not let low self-esteem tell me I am not good enough or smart enough to do the task.

Oh no, today I will not let self hinder me or break my stride because I can do *all things* with the

Lord on my side.

CHAPTER FIVE
INTERNAL CONFLICT:
PULLING OFF THE MASKS

Do you feel as if you're in conflict with yourself? That is exactly how I felt when I first met the stranger, I was hiding behind my masks. For a long time, the masks were my security blanket. It took me months to embrace the person in the mirror without the masks. Taking them off meant I had to be vulnerable and let others see the real me, that was a daunting and scary feeling. The reason I put the mask on in the first place was so that others could not see me; even though I had seen a glimpse of that beautiful person God showed me, I still was not ready to disrobe. Has the Holy Spirit ever told you something and someone came along and confirmed what God had said? That is exactly what happened to me.

"It is okay to be who you are, it does not matter who likes or accepts you, as long as you are being true to who God called you to be."

Even though I knew I needed to take the masks off for good, for fear of acceptance and being judged, while at work, I was a different person from who I naturally was at home. I would not let my true personality shine through, I never let my co-workers see the real LaSandra. I remember one of my co-workers telling me one day, 'It is okay to be who you are, it does not matter who likes or accepts you, as long as you are being true to who God called you to be.' At that moment, I was set free! I was free to let my light shine and display the true me.

A week after that conversation, my company hosted a company-wide conference where they invited a guest motivational speaker in to inspire us. I sat on the front row, because there were no other seats available. It seems as if there is always a vacant seat in the front row just for me – it's God's way of setting me up. After the conference was over the speaker stopped me as I was walking out of the room. He told me my aura was very bright and that the light around me was vibrant. Someone else chimed in and said she could see my light also. He went further to ask me, 'What is God calling you to do?' Honestly, I could not answer him. I had written the inspirational devotional but that was just to help me get through being separated from Kelvin. However, I never connected that to my purpose. At that moment, I began to wonder what my calling was and how could I find out.

That night I went home and asked my husband, 'Do you ever wonder why we are here? I mean is there more to life than just going to work and coming home.' After that conversation to help me on my quest, my husband bought me a book about discovering your purpose and told me to read it. He also suggested I start going back to Sunday School if I did not know my purpose. From that day forward, my goal was to find out what my purpose was so that I could be fulfilled.

That experience taught me how to take the mask off once and for all. You and I are going to go through the steps so that you too can take your mask off for good!

Step One: The first step is denying self. That is right, you cannot please self and God at the same time. When we keep the mask on, we are saying to God, we (His creation) are not perfect and we must alter ourselves by covering what we believe are imperfections. But guess what, what we see as imperfection is actually what Christ uses to draw others to him. I can attest the time I spent running away from the fact that I was the victim of circumstance which was no fault of my own, albeit a traumatic experience, I made it. I had faced many adversities, it was not easy growing up in a home without a father, but my mother raised three successful women in spite of that fact. We were walking testimonies but because of my own insecurities, I did not see it that way. Now God is using the very things I saw as weaknesses as a platform for his kingdom. Isn't it ironic, those things I covered for years, and those painful experiences would be the platform God would have me to use to help others? To do this, I had to deny myself of self-pity, that is, feeling sorry for myself so that I could take the mask off for good.

Step Two: I understood the importance being vulnerable. What do I mean by being vulnerable? I mean, I had to be myself, no matter what and accept that I am not for everyone. Sometimes that meant I would not fit in with others. For whatever reason, everyone is not going to like you and guess what? That is okay. Ironically enough, these individuals are going through something themselves and their rejection of you has nothing to do with you. Let me say it again, people who are not accepting of you are battling their own demons, and they either see something in you God gave you and they desire it, they are jealous or just plain not happy with who they are. That has nothing to do with you.

Have you ever been told someone does not like you, but ·they do not even know you? Let me free you, it is not you, it is them. That person is dealing with their own issues and insecurities. Do not let that hinder you from being the person God knew before He formed you in your mother's womb. If you are not careful, people will cause you to second guess, who you are in an effort to please them. Your purpose is to please God and not man.

Step Three: Finally, it took acceptance. I had to learn that I could not change my past. The behavior and actions I did before that moment, I needed to take ownership and responsibility. I needed to repent and rebuke the enemy when he tried to remind me of who I once was. When God forgives us, He remembers our sin no more. Therefore, do not let anyone remind you of what you did in the past, this includes yourself. Accepting Jesus Christ means you are washed in His blood and free from your past actions. Jesus forgave you, so, release. Do not torture yourself or let others torture you either. Remember, scripture tells us in John 8:36 (ESV), "So if the Son sets you free, you will be free indeed."

Unknowingly, I was comfortable hiding behind my masks as protective shields. I hid my true identity from my co-workers because I believed I needed to act a certain way to be accepted. My co-worker literally set me free the day she told me it was okay to be who I really was. Now I do not take it personal when who I am does not fit in someone else's limited opinions of me because I know the spirit living in them is in conflict with the Holy Spirit that resides in me. When that guest speaker asked me, 'What was God calling me to do?', I was dumbfounded. That question prompted me to investigate my purpose. Unfortunately, I did not realize writing and inspiring others was my purpose. Self-acceptance and vulnerability are needed when pulling off your mask.

Now we have moved past internally fighting within yourself, how are you feeling? I hope you feel a sense of excitement because you are making strides in becoming the person God intended you to be all along. That person who was born with purpose.

BREAKING STRONGHOLDS

My physical body and mind are somewhat in coherent.

My soul and my spirit crave something different.

I'm walking and wondering what to do next.

My thoughts are here and there I am so perplexed.

I hear a faint knock at the door of my heart.

A voice saying, "I can give you a new start."

Tears rundown my face as I cry out "Lord is it You?"

But Satan steps in and taunts me saying "Jesus Who?"

Jesus knocks again and says "My child take my hand,

I will give you the strength you need to stand."

As I wrestle with my doubts and fears to grab hold.

Satan tries to tighten his stronghold.

He shows me all the things I must leave behind.

I look to Jesus who tells me, "I can give you peace of mind."

CHAPTER SIX
WHO IS GOD CALLING YOU TO BE?

Years ago, someone asked me, 'Who are you?' She asked me this question as I shared with her a business venture I wanted to pursue. In an effort to help me write a mission and vision statement, she needed me to go further in depth. But I was stomped by that question and I could not answer it. I did not know who I was or what I was supposed to be doing. Sadly, I did not pursue that business venture because I could not answer the question. I felt I could not be a value to anyone not knowing who I was or where I was going.

I am not without faults and flaws, none of us are without blemish. The difference between then and now, is now I know who I am, and I have learned to totally embrace myself. My imperfections are what make me unique! The revelation of who I am, was self-evident when I reflected over my life from a different perspective. I have been knocked down more times than I can count but by God's grace and mercy, I have always gotten back up again. Have you ever heard that old adage, *"You can't keep a good girl down?"* Those words were never truer for me. When I look back over my life, I can take inventory of all the times I had the wind knocked out of me. With each storm there is evidence that I have always risen again with every blow. God had his hands on me all the time, even during the times I was doing things that were not pleasing in His sight. As I said, I am a faithful perseverer and mighty in the Lord. Through countless of conversations with Jesus, tears and soul searching, I finally discovered who I am.

I want to challenge you with the same questions that was asked of me, "Who are you?" Pause and think about it for just a moment. Has your mask been shattered yet? Are you starting to see the person God is calling you to be? Are you beginning to gain clarity?

Isaiah 40:29 says, *The Lord gives strength to the weary and increases the power of the weak.* You may feel as if you are not strong enough or equipped with what you need to answer your call, but I want you to know that our Father has equipped you with what you need to start and as you grow spiritually stronger in Him, He will add to it. I know all too well about feeling under qualified, I too was once in your shoes but what I realized was I could either surrender or keep running. Funny thing about taking off the mask and being empowered; it reveals the truth. Empowerment! What a wonderful privilege to receive, and that is exactly what we have in Christ.

When I finally realized who I was, it was invigorating, I felt a sigh of relief. For years, I hid this beautiful person from the world and when I discovered the newfound person, I was empowered. By answering the call and accepting who you are in Him, He gives you the authority to overcome all the things that seek to have you question what you should be doing, that is your calling. No matter how hard you try, the truth has a way of catching up to you, meaning you can run for so long, but after a while the truth will slap you in the face. And that is exactly what happened to me, I was running when I put on those masks, God allowed me to go so far and after a while, I had no choice but to remove the masks, and embrace who God called me to be. I was free, I had been delivered.

> *"When on your quest to find who God is calling you to be, a divine shift must occur in your thinking, which should manifest in your subsequent actions."*

As with anything, spiritual deliverance comes with a price. Not everyone will embrace the new you. In fact, they will seek to keep the labels you are escaping from on you because the old you is more relatable to them. The person you were is more comfortable for them. However, you need to focus your attention and efforts on who our Creator is calling you to be. Once He reveals to you who you are in Him, it is difficult to continue denying and ignoring that you are unique, and God set you aside just for Him. No matter how hard you try, that inner voice within will gently remind you of your value and worth.

It had been four years after my husband and I reconciled, and our marriage was well on its way in our recovery journey. God did not only restore our marriage, He made our relationship even better. Ironically enough, I was still writing inspirational messages, but it was to encourage others as well as myself. God gives us information in pieces, you see, He knows that spiritually we cannot comprehend all that He has to say to us in one setting, so He uses other means to get His message to us. In other words, sometimes He speaks through others to let you know what His plans are for you. Now, the caveat is, you have to be in a position to receive. Oftentimes we discount what someone tells us because we do not like the way they look or feel, they are not qualified to tell us anything. Keep this in mind, the Father can and will use anyone to get His message to you. Our qualifications and God's qualifications are totally different. He qualifies those willing to be used for His purpose. Sometimes, God uses those who you do not have a relationship with, while other times He will use those you are familiar with, whatever the medium, He has a way of getting your attention.

Have you ever noticed how God shows up in the strangest places to reveal His plan for you? One morning, I was standing at the coffee machine at work when a co-worker walked up to me and asked if I was a motivational speaker. I told him no, I am sure he could tell I was puzzled by the look on my face. He told me he had a dream about me the night before where I was on stage getting ready to speak but the room was dark, and the doors were locked. He went on to say that I was in this room with people of great authority holding high positions. He characterized these people as "*bad actors*", he told me the auditorium was full and the attendees had to use lighters to find their seats. He went on to say, when I started talking light could be seen all around me. He then interpreted the dream for me. His gift was interpreting dreams like Joseph in the Bible. He told me that I would have the audiences of people in high places and that God was going to elevate me where I would have an influence over them. This was one of three prophecies he shared with me. The reason why this seemed strange, was because before that day, I had never had a conversation with this person, I would always be cordial and speak but we never engaged and in any type of banter. I knew immediately, the Holy Spirit was using him to tell me who Jesus was calling me to be. I mean, beyond a shadow of doubt, I knew God was answering the question, that I had been seeking an answer for, that is, what is my purpose for being on Earth. That evening when I got home, I began to ponder what my co-worker told me. I prayed that night asking God what His plan was for my life. In the days to come ahead, I began writing poems and really delving deeper into His word, my mission was to discover if my secret desire to speak publicly was what God was calling me to do.

When on your quest to find your purpose, a divine shift must occur in your thinking, which should manifest in your subsequent actions. Ephesians 4: 22-24 tells us, "To put off your old self, which belongs to your former manner of life and is corrupt through deceitful desires, and to be renewed in the spirit of your minds, and to put on the new self, created after the likeness of God in true righteousness and holiness." By taking off your mask you are transforming yourself, moving away from your old way of thinking and living into a new person taking on Godly thinking and behavior. Remember, God is setting you aside for His purpose and in doing so, you have to leave your mask behind. This is exactly what happened to me, my thoughts of who I was shifted and I no longer was the person who needed a mask as security. In order for me to embrace my calling I needed to be open, honest, and transparent about where He was leading me. My friend, you will have to do the same. My co-worker did not know it or maybe he did, but God had just given me a glimpse of the woman I was to be in Christ and He will do the same thing for you. Open your heart and mind spiritually to receive His revelation of who He is calling you to be, that purpose He created you to fulfill.

Are you starting to see the divine plan for you? Can you see who Christ is calling you to be? If you cannot, not to worry it will come in time. If patience is not your strong suit, get ready because you will develop patience going through this process. But as you wait patiently, stay in constant prayer and meditation, seeking God's guidance. Be careful of who you get advice from, people may mean well and have no ill-intention but all things considered, all advice is not Godly and can thwart you from finding out who you are being called to be. Everyone does not have the spirit of discernment or prophecy and should not be allowed to speak over you. In this stage of the process, you must be very careful who you allow to speak into and over you. Life and death lies in the tongue and as someone newly seeking to take off a mask, the last thing you need or want is for the enemy to creep in and plague your mind with thoughts contrary to what God has already showed you.

The quest to find out who you are and what you should be doing in Christ is a journey. You will need to transform your thinking and change your perspective. Unveiling the person behind the mask, means facing the truth. This can be daunting, but it is necessary. Be encouraged in knowing there is a freedom that comes with accepting what was (your past) to move towards what is to come (your future). The masks I wore served as a hinderance. It prevented me from being who God intended me to be and hid me from the world. Along the way you may hear things such as, "I liked the old you better." or "You are different, I don't like it," that is to be expected. Some in your inner circle prefer you to stay the same and do the same things. On the contrary, to fully embrace who you are in Christ, you must let go of your old way of doing things. Sometimes, God uses others to tell you His plan or confirm what He has already told you. Do not miss the message because you feel that person is not qualified to guide you. God in His sovereignty can use anyone and anything.

Before we move on, I encourage you to seek God with your whole heart and ask Him what His purpose and plan for your life is. This may not be revealed overnight, God works in His appointed time, not ours. If we are not where we need to be spiritually, He will delay revealing certain information to us until we are ready.

A WOMAN OF GOD!

There is more to me than what meets the eye

I am a woman with character, integrity, and a beautiful smile

And because I have Christ, I am free from sin

My Godly ways make me attractive in ways you cannot comprehend

I am a woman who's on a quest to reach her destiny

Why? Because my Father has laid out my path before me

I am a woman who is guided by the Holy Spirit

My communion with Jesus keeps me from becoming weary

There is more to me than you will ever fully understand

I am equipped with His power that gives me the strength to withstand

A woman of inner strength, love, peace, and wisdom

These things empower and encourage me to be a Godly being

I can embrace who my Father called me to be

A Woman of God, Yes that's me!

CHAPTER SEVEN
SPIRITUAL SELF-DISCOVERY

I should tell you that some of the masks you wore may have been tied to evil spirits and to fully be free from those masks you are going to have to fight even harder in the spiritual realm. That is, you are going to have to come against those spirits with the Word of God. For me, the spirit of fornication, the spirit of bitterness, and the spirit of darkness to name a few were upon me. I now know, God delivered me straight from the hands of the enemy. As long as I was living in sin and hiding behind the mask, I was not a threat to the enemy because I was not serving in my divine purpose. You are not a threat to Satan, as long as you are living a life of sin because you are operating on the enemy's side against God. I had to hide the word of God in my heart and you will have to do the same so that you too can be free. Doing so, helps me maintain a Godly attitude and lifestyle, preventing me from putting the masks back on. Hiding the word of God in your heart will also help you maintain a Godly spirit arming you with what you need to fight off evil spirits.

One important thing to note is that God wants you to surrender to His will. In one of the earlier chapter's I told you, during one of my conversations with God, I gave him every facet of my life. I surrendered to Him and His will. This is important and necessary because He needs to know that you are relinquishing your life to Him and following His lead and not your own. I was tired, I had done it my way for too long, getting nowhere. I knew there was something more to my life than what I was doing and I wanted to know what that was so I could be fulfilled. Before God will reveal your purpose to you, He has to know you are totally His. You must give yourself to Him completely. Think about it, would you reveal your most intimate secrets to someone who is not committed to you? In the same way, if you are not all in with God, He will withhold that which concerns His kingdom from you.

As you spend time with our Heavenly Father, studying His word, in aligning yourself with Him, you will begin to develop an intimate relationship with Him. In time, the Lord will begin to show you His plan for you and how you will serve in the body of Christ. This means, He will show you, your role in His kingdom. Remember, your purpose could very well be something that you have been doing all along but did not realize it was your calling. When God reveals Himself and His plans to you, I encourage you to take notes of your conversations and revelations. Doing this will help you remember key things He has told you. It will also allow you to meditate and pray on them in the coming days so that you can receive clarity and guidance on exactly what it is He wants you to do.

When God reveals to you who you are in the body of Christ, the role you will serve (your purpose) will soon follow. Your purpose is closely tied to what you are passionate about. For me, I find passion in encouraging, empowering, and inspiring others to see themselves as Christ sees them. Most often, our purpose in life is birthed out of tragedy, some sort of painful experience. In my case, I had experienced loss at an early age, date rape, and many broken relationships which led to me questioning my existence. I once saw a movie where one of the characters asked her best friend, *"Are you living or are you existing?"* that question resonated with me. Right when that movie was released, I was going through this very process of finding my purpose. During that time, I literally focused my attention on finding out what my purpose was in

Christ.

> *"A man's gift makes room for him and brings him before great men."*
> *Proverbs 18:16 (NKJV)*

When we are born, our Heavenly Father gives us at least one gift. He gives us this gift because He wants us to use it to glorify Him. Now, what do I mean when I say gift? I mean the thing that you do which comes natural to you. You do not have to work hard at doing it, it is as if you were born to do it. Guess what? You were. You see the thing that you are really good at doing, is what you should be doing for God's kingdom. As I told you earlier, I am a natural at writing and encouraging others and I find great joy in it. Wherever I go, I am always smiling and saying good morning, afternoon or evening. I am the person that asks you how you are doing and really want to know, and if by chance you tell me you are not doing so well, I will give you a word of encouragement. I remember one evening while attending graduate school, passing this young lady in the hallway as I was heading to the restroom. She looked very sad. I told her, her dress was pretty and the color really looked nice on her. She responded, "Thanks, that is the nicest thing anyone has said to me today," she smiled and then said, "You just made my day." She walked away with a smile on her face and it made me feel good to know I had given her encouragement.

It was during those days of isolation from my marriage

and the world that I would talk to God, asking him what His plan was for my life. And, then it hit me, all along I was already doing it. For years, I have been encouraging and motivating others verbally and through my writings, I just did not realize it was my calling. At that moment, I knew all of those devotionals I wrote during my separation from my husband was not for me to keep to myself, they were to encourage others who were faced with similar issues and needed a spiritual pick me up or a prayer because they did not have the words or courage to talk to God. My writings were what others needed to know, God was with them and there was hope in their situation or whatever it was they were going through. Your journey to discovering your purpose may not be identical to mine, do not get frustrated or give up. God does not work on our time, He works on His own timing.

Many people quote the scripture, "The spirit is willing, but the flesh is weak." (Matthew 26:41) Well, aligning your will with that of Christ is allowing him to direct you. This can be difficult for you when things are not moving at the pace you believe they should be moving. Remember, when I told you that I took things into my own hands and filed for a divorce even though I had this funny feeling I should not do it? Doing so caused me to fall out of alignment with God. I know, we live in a microwave society, everything is instantaneous. Guess what, things do not always happen suddenly, sometimes God will delay things to ensure you are spiritually ready to receive what He has for you. Aligning yourself with Christ is critical, not just for finding your purpose, but also to live a Godly life. The sole reason you are seeking your purpose is so that you can serve in the body of Christ. To serve in the body of Christ, you must be aligned with Him and willing to follow His lead. Aligning yourself to Christ is allowing the Holy Spirit to lead you and teach you. You are exhibiting your faith and trust in God by doing so.

In Jeremiah, God tells us, "Before you were formed in your mother's womb he knew you; He pointed out he knows the plans he has for us, plans to prosper us and give us hope and a future"(Jeremiah 1:5; 29:11 NIV). This means the Lord knew how He was going to use you in His Kingdom before you were even conceived. He made you for His purpose and had specific plans for you even back then during conception.

What an honor it is to know God created me and you with a purposeful plan in mind. Now, it is very difficult to understand and serve in your purpose without full alignment with Christ. Sure, you can use your gift to make money but that is not serving God's purpose, it is serving yours. To serve Him, you must be willing to commit your gift to His will for the furtherance of His Kingdom here on Earth. A lot of people get caught in serving themselves with their gift, I do not want you to fall in this category. It is easy to do, but if you are committed to pleasing God and are aligned to His will, like mine, your desire will be to please Him with your gift.

Perception is the belief of one's own reality (your point of view); spiritual perspective is looking at things from Christ's point of view. Let's take my gift of writing for example. Now I could essentially use this talent for personal gain, I mean, there is a niche for writing all sorts of things, but that does not necessarily mean it would benefit the body of Christ. On the other hand, by me writing this book, I am encouraging you and other readers to see yourselves like Christ, embracing who you are, so that you can shed the mask you have been wearing and walk in purpose. What's my point? Discovering your purpose is one thing, but how you use it is something entirely different. Before I discovered my purpose, I would write all the time but just for my amusement, it did not benefit the kingdom. I wrote poems, songs, short stories, I even started a fictional book. But none of what I wrote was at the caliber of writing I do today, because Christ was not in it. When you use your gift for Christ's kingdom, God will enhance your talent. I am always amazed at the things I write, and I always credit it to the Holy Spirit writing through me. Having a spiritual perspective allows you to understand the significance of using your gift from a kingdom point of view.

Your purpose may not be revealed to you in one day, my purpose certainly was not. I had to surrender to God, and you do too. Ask God, what is your purpose and how you can use it to benefit His kingdom. It is impossible to serve God without aligning to His will. Without spiritual alignment serving in the body of Christ is very difficult. Having the mindset of Christ is essential to serving in His body, it lends spiritual perspective and helps you to develop the skill of thinking Godly. Using your gifts for the Kingdom of God is the sole reason He created you. We all could find other ways to use our gifts for our own personal gain, but only what we do for Christ will last. God set you aside and gave you that gift for a reason, to glorify Him.

Before we move on to the next chapter, I want you to answer these questions:

1. Are you willing to surrender to God?

2. Can you identify something that you are good at doing?

3. What is it that you do that brings you joy, and you feel as if time is standing still when you do it?

4. Are you willing to align with Christ and use your gift to

help others?

5. What perspective do you have about your purpose and how it will benefit the kingdom?

These questions will help you discover your motives. God looks at our hearts and if our hearts are not right, it does not matter what we do or how often, He will not recognize our efforts. Using your gift for self-gratification is just as bad as not using it all. Neither benefit the Kingdom of God. The questions above serve as a tool for you to survey your motives, thus revealing what is in your heart.

CHAPTER EIGHT
IN TUNE WITH THE SPIRIT

Having a Godly mindset is to be in tune with the Holy Spirit. Do not be afraid of the Holy Spirit. Consider it your navigational system, your God Positioning System (GPS) so to speak. The Holy Spirit directs, guides, and leads you according to the instructions of our Heavenly Father. I never prayed as hard as I prayed after separating from my husband. But reflecting back, I was developing my prayer and meditation life, which is extremely important for serving in my calling. When serving in your purpose you will need to be in constant contact with our Heavenly Father, which means you need to get comfortable with praying and talking to Him.

I am in constant contact with Him about my assignments, challenges I may face, and everything else going on in my life. This is a routine you will need to adopt as well. You should get into the habit of setting aside time to talk to God and meditate on His words daily. You will always need His guidance, navigation, and resources as you serve in His purpose for your life. There will be times when you need God to clear the path for you and other times you will need Him to show you the path and give you clarity.

To fully understand your purpose, you must be harmonious with Him. Retreating in the Lord is my refuge! Why? Because the deeper I go in Him, the more intimate our relationship becomes. The more intimate our relationship becomes, the more compliant I become with what He wants me to do in my purpose. It is true nothing can separate us from the love of Christ, but to experience this type of love from Him, you must spend time getting to know Him on a deeper level, and getting to know His plans for you. This should be your goal as well. You should have a genuine desire to want to serve in your purpose. Imagine, having a love interest and wanting to get to know him intimately, how much time would you spend with that person to learn everything you could about him, his likes, his dislikes, his interests, and his plans? In the same way, Christ desires the same level of commitment and dedication you would devote to getting to know others to get to know Him. During your prayer time ask, God, how do I serve You? What is it You want me to do? In time, He will give you all the answers you need to understand His plan for you.

> *Being in tune with the spirit means you know the voice of God."*

One of my prayers even still today is for spiritual discernment. You have to be able to discern when God is speaking to you versus when the enemy is speaking to you. As I said, I am in constant communication with Jesus, every day, all day. There is so much going on around me and I do not want to get distracted and lose focus of Him or my purpose. Being able to discern when God is leading you comes with knowing the voice of God. The more time you spend with Him, the more accustom you will become to hearing His voice. Every morning when I rise, before my feet touch the ground, I pray and welcome the Holy Spirit. My commute to work is my praise and worship time, this is when I converse with God. Because I communicate with God, I know His voice. Let me ask you a question, think of someone very close to you, if they called you from afar, would you know their voice? I am guessing as they moved closer to you (in ear shot) you could discern the voice. Well, God wants you to know when He is speaking to you as well. Being in tune with the spirit means you know God's voice. You should get comfortable with talking to God, as you do the more comfortable you will become in His presence, the easier it would be to heed His voice.

Now your relationship with Christ does not become intimate overnight. Just as it takes time to develop an intimate relationship with a significant other, it takes time to do so with Christ too. Intimate relationships take time, commitment, and patience. Trust the process of developing your relationship with Jesus. We are fortunate enough to have a road map, which serves as our guide to all things we need to know about Christ, the Bible. The Bible is God's love letter to us. Reading it reveals His nature, His desire and purpose, it gives us spiritual insight. As I said earlier, spiritual insight is useful when seeking to understand how you will operate in the body of Christ.

"Submit yourselves therefore to God. Resist the devil and he will flee from you."(James 4:7 ESV) Submitting to God's will is a conscious decision we must make daily. I mentioned in the previous chapter, I had to surrender to God in order to serve in my purpose. Submitting to God is the act of surrendering your will to His, meaning, coming into agreement and obedience to His commands and will for your life.

In order to fulfill your purpose, you must make up in your mind that you are going to abdicate your will and embrace the will of God for your life. For me it was easy to do, I knew, I was living outside the will of God and took control from Him. I made decisions based on my lens. I had been making all the wrong decisions for myself. As a result, I made a lot of bad decisions that could have been avoided if I had allowed God to lead me from the beginning. You will have to make a decision as well, to submit to God, letting him take the lead and guide you. It is the only way you can effectively serve in the body of Christ. Both of you cannot lead, since God is not going to submit to your will, you must be the one to submit to His. It is impossible to please Elohim (God) if you are unwilling to submit to Him and be obedient. Submission requires obedience. Obedience to His word, commands, instructions, and so forth. Let's go back to when I filed for divorce but in my gut, I knew I should not have and I kept getting this strange feeling that it was not the right thing to do. That was the Holy Spirit nudging me, telling me that I was going against God's will.

Reflect back to a time you decided to do something and got the feeling you should not do it. What was the outcome? Did it work out for you, or did it make your situation worse? Fortunately for me, I did not go through with the divorce and listened to God's instructions. Scripture tells us in I Samuel 15, that obedience is better than sacrifice and one thing is for sure, to be in tuned with the Holy Spirit is to hearken to God's instruction. Did you know your blessings are tied to your obedience? Well, they are, throughout the Bible God instructs us regarding what he wants us to do and if we honor His command, He will bless us. A good example is shown in Psalms 37:14, "Delight yourself in the Lord and He will give you the desires of your heart." This scripture tells us if we exalt God, He will bless us with what we desire.

To be in tune with the Holy Spirit means listening to that

inner voice when it speaks to your consciousness and adhering to what you heard. Being in tune means allowing the Spirit to lead you in all decisions whether big or small, so that everything you do glorifies God. Your gift was given to you for just that, to glorify God and benefit others. An unwillingness to submit means there is an unwillingness to be obedient to the will of our Lord and Savior, and will be impossible for you to fulfill your purpose.

A Godly mindset and a willingness to surrender and submit will help you to be obedient to the will of God and prepare you for the days ahead as you get into position to serve in your purpose.

Before we move on, I want you to ask God to survey your heart. Ask Him if there is anything preventing you from surrendering to Him. Let Him know that you are committed to Him, willing to surrender and submit to Him, and have the desire to be in tune with His Spirit.

AWAKENING

I'm walking in my divine purpose, finally found my place in this world.

No longer hunted from things that happened to me as a little girl.

I have forgiven my mother and others for their trespasses against me.

Embracing the path God has placed before me,

I now know the woman I am to be,

Encouraging others during their troubles, that is my ministry.

I surrendered all to Jesus to have a life filled with joy and peace.

Freedom from the pain and the key was forgiveness in order for me to increase.

I now know talking to Jesus makes everything alright.

No longer do I battle with evil because He's got this fight.

Many may wonder how I overcame the darkness in my world,

I prayed, the Holy Spirit filled me, then I danced and I

twirled,

You see, as I was focused on the problem, the enemy crept in and plagued my thoughts,

But now I have stride in my walk and pep in my talk because it was Jesus I sought.

From now on I will forever remain spiritually strong,

Because I know one thing is for sure; there is safety in His arms!

Chapter Nine
Mission Critical

This is your Heavenly Father speaking, welcome to Mission Control, where the Holy Spirit will be your comforter and guide on your purpose driven journey! Your mission, should you choose to accept it, is to follow Jesus and serve in your purpose. The Holy Spirit will serve as your guide as you walk in divine purpose and fulfill your tasks as assigned. Along the way on this journey, you will face challenges, obstacles, and setbacks, but not to worry. I Yahweh (God) will be with you every step of the way.

There will be times when you will need others, resources and tools to complete your assignment, do not be concerned, I, your Heavenly Father have set aside everything that you need and it will be given to you, in it's appointed time. I have placed them strategically in various locations and you will receive them as your journey takes you to where I have ordained you to go. I and I alone, will preserve you during this journey. You will be my servant and I will be your God, guiding you and comforting you every step of the way. When others try to come against you, I will fight your battles. You have been armed with my armor and must wear it daily. Your assignment should you choose to accept it will not always be easy, but I have assigned an angel to protect you. Will you accept your assignment?

> *"Your gifts will encourage and help others to understand, I have a divine purpose for them."*

Should you decide not to fulfill your purpose, the Holy Spirit will remind you frequently of your mission. It is critical that you accept my will and this mission. There are others who are waiting on you to fulfill your purpose so that they can fulfill theirs. Your gifts will encourage and help others to understand, I too have a divine purpose for them. For it is written, *"Before I formed you in the womb I knew you, before you were born I set you apart; I appointed you as a prophet to the nations."* Jeremiah 1:5. You cannot run from your purpose or my will, at some point, you will have to accept your mission and serve me.

Allow me to give you a great example of how your purpose is tied to others. It was a Sunday school lesson that was taught to me in my youth. Remember, the Prophet Jonah? He attempted to run away from his assignment, but in the end he had to submit to the will of God. The story goes, God told Jonah to go to Nineveh and preach against their sin. Jonah refused the assignment and went to another city to buy a one-way ticket for a boat to head in the opposite direction of where God instructed him to go. One of the reasons Jonah did not want to go to Nineveh was because he was afraid. While Jonah was on the boat, God caused a great storm to occur which threatened to destroy the boat. In an effort to save themselves the sailors threw Jonah overboard when they realized he was the reason why God was angry. God prepared a whale to swallow Jonah and inside the belly he stayed for three days and three nights. During Jonah's isolation inside the whale he prayed, and God commanded the whale to vomit Jonah up on dry land. Jonah then went to Nineveh to fulfill his mission. Because Jonah fulfilled his purpose, the people of Nineveh were saved. God's will, will always be done. (Read Jonah 1-4).

Like Jonah, God caused a great storm (separation from my husband) to occur in my life to get my attention. During those days of isolation from my husband and family, I too prayed like Jonah seeking God's face. He had a plan for me all along, and all those things I experienced pushed me towards my purpose. It was not by happenstance that I would write daily to encourage myself day-in-day-out, I faced separation from my husband, family and wandered aimlessly in the wilderness. Those moments were a part of God's plan to bring me back to Him and fulfill my purpose using the gifts God gave me to serve him and help others. Like Jonah, I was afraid. I was afraid to show people who I was, so I piled on many masks. Those masks served to prevent me from walking in my purpose for all of those years. Suddenly, I hit a brick wall and had no choice but to discard the masks, embrace who God had called me to be, and serve in my purpose. In a sense, I was hiding from the Lord, or so I thought.

What is your mission? What is it God is calling you to do? Will you choose to accept it? For me, it was motivating and inspiring others. It was actually something I was already doing but now I was going to do it for the Lord. "And whatever you do or say, do it as a representative of the Lord Jesus, giving thanks through him to God the Father." (Colossians 3:17 NIV). I accepted my mission and the Holy Spirit has been guiding me ever since. Will you let the Holy Spirit guide you too? I know, you may be afraid, because you feel you do not know where to start or what to do. But rest assured, all you need is to believe in Christ and He will show you what to do, just like He shows me even now.

I am not going to tell you that all of my days are rosy or that this journey has been a piece of cake, because I would not be telling the truth. Accepting your mission puts you on the front line for Christ, but also exposes you to the enemy. Now, what do I mean by that? I mean when you walk in purpose, you are the agent Jesus uses to help others. The enemy does not want you to follow Christ or serve in your purpose helping others, doing so only serves to expand the body of Christ. The enemy's job is to steal, kill, and destroy (John 10:10). That means, preventing you from fulfilling your purpose. This is the reason, God has assigned an angel to protect you, His job is to shield you from the attacks and schemes of the enemy.

The enemy's goal is to destroy the body of Christ and all those who are a part of it. I am not telling you this to scare you, deter you from following Christ or serving in your purpose. My intent is to let you know that though the Holy Spirit is guiding you and will comfort you, the enemy will innately come after you. You can do anything through Christ, and God will give you what you need to carry out your divine assignments and walk in your purpose. But as God instructed you, you must put on the armor He gave you so that you can fight effectively in the spirit coming against the enemy in truth. The word of God is your sword. Knowing God's word and using it properly will cause the enemy to flee.

Let me give you some context to what I am saying. In 2011, a friend of mine was having an event and her keynote speaker canceled at the last minute. She called me and asked me to speak. This was my very first time speaking, and I was super excited. I loved speaking and it came so natural to me. By then I had realized speaking and motivating others was my calling and what better way for me to use my gift of encouragement than speaking in front of an audience. I accepted her invitation to speak and that event was a huge success. That same year, I received a call from a playwright who commissioned me to write poems for her screenplay. That was awesome as well, but after the debut of the play, she wrote my poems out of the script. I was saddened by her decision, but I kept the faith because I believed and trusted God. Fast forward to 2018, I received two invitations to speak at two separate church engagements. They both were canceled. I was disappointed, I asked God, "Why did both of them cancel?" He gently whispered, "Because, I do not want anyone saying they gave you your start as a motivational speaker, I want you to plan a conference and debut yourself as a motivational speaker."

On June 22, 2019, I hosted my first conference and it was a huge success. Do you see my point? Even in setbacks God has a plan for you and no one or nothing can thwart His plan. But you must keep the faith, stay focused on God and your purpose, follow the Holy Spirit and things will fall in place. Now if I had not had a relationship with God and knew I could take Him at His word, I probably would have just wallowed in defeat when those conferences were canceled. Here is what I am telling you, do not doubt God or yourself. You are everything Christ says you are! If you only believe, by now you should be well on your way to accepting who Christ is calling you to be, pulling off the masks and ready to walk into your divine destiny.

There are a number of things that you could be called to

do. For instance, you can be an encourager, intercessor (praying for others), teacher, singer, financial guru, caregiver, the list goes on and on. No matter the call, one thing is for sure, God gave you a gift and He intended for you to use it for His purpose. I know it can be daunting to put yourself out there. You may have a lot of questions. What if I am not good enough or what if people do not want my help? But what if you were born for your assigned mission? What if your mission is exactly what people needed? The point I am making is, God picked you for a reason. Let me assure you accepting your mission, helping others in the kingdom, is very rewarding. I take solace in knowing every time I share an encouraging word with someone, I am fulfilling my mission. You too can experience that awesome feeling of helping someone with your gift. Are you ready to fulfill your purpose? Daily I ask God to use me as His instrument, essentially, I am telling Him to use my gifts for His purpose. You see, I am a just the willing vessel He uses to help others. The operative phrase is *"willing vessel"* you have to be willing to let Him use you? Ask God to search your heart, remove all fear and anything that is preventing you from serving in the Kingdom, using your gift.

Your mission is so important, God chose you to carry it out! What an honor it is for you to be chosen to serve God's most prized creation; His people. I want you to understand this, that your gift and what you do with it should serve God and not yourself. Sure, a byproduct of you following Christ and using your gifts is that you will be blessed. But your focus should be glorifying God and edifying His people. When you lose sight of the objective, you will start to serve yourself rather than God. Doing this will displease Him and cause you to live outside of His will for you; and, you have already been down that road, I do not have to tell you it is a dead-end.

While operating in your purpose you must be careful, because the enemy will try to persuade you to do things alternatively to what God wants you to do. The enemy is cunning, and he will attempt to impart thoughts in you that seem to be reasonable. Take those devotions I wrote to minister to myself for instance, when I would share them, people were telling me I need to put them in book form and publish it, but I would always say, 'no they are for me.' The Holy Spirit was trying to tell me what God wanted me to do. I did not receive it, because of the selfish thoughts I had that they were only for me. The enemy knew that if I published a devotional book, God would be glorified and others would be helped, possibly even accepting Christ in their lives. It was wrong of me to think I was writing only to help myself recover from what I was going through, when there were others like me who were hurt too, for one reason or another.

Are you starting to see why it is so critical for you to accept the mission? Your personality and gifts are unique to you. Sure, someone else may sing but she may not have the compassion and flair that you have. Let's revisit the story of Jonah, yes, God could have chosen someone else to prophesy to the Ninevites, but He chose Jonah for a reason. Jonah was a good man and God's prophet. God has also chosen you and purposed you to be a blessing to others.

Your Kingdom mission is critical. Your gifts are unique to you and your personality. Accepting it will please God and help others that are waiting on you. God has purposed you to do His works and those works serve to minister to others. God's GPS will serve to guide you as you follow the Holy Spirit. The Holy Spirit will comfort, guide, and lead you. Remember, the enemy will not be pleased that you are serving in your purpose. He will seek to distract and hinder you from serving in your purpose. The armor of God serves as your protective shield and will allow you to fight in spirit and truth. Throughout the Bible there were many who answered the call, and now God is summoning you to take your rightful position in His army.

Before we move on, think about your mission? Are you willing to accept it? Are you willing to follow the guidance of the Holy Spirit? Are you willing to deny your self will and pursue the will of God? You must answer these questions in all earnest and honesty because in the days to come some will cause you to doubt yourself, lose faith, and question your faith. During these days you will have to remember the objective, stay prayerful, and maintain your faith and trust in Jesus. You must be strong enough in Christ to fight off the wiles of the enemy and continue on in your purpose. The only way to fight effectively, will be putting on the armor God gave you, so that you can fight in spirit and truth of His Holy Word.

Chapter Ten
Planning For Your Debut

Congratulations, you have committed to God and accepted your mission to use your gift for His Kingdom. Are you excited? You should be ecstatic about your transformation into the person God has called you to be and that you are ready to serve in your divine purpose. Everyone will not be on board with what God has instructed you to do. Do not get discouraged. Keep in mind, when you share the vision God gave you, everyone will not agree or understand. I repeat everyone will not embrace what God is leading you to do or where He is leading you, and that is okay. He did not give the vision to them, He gave it to you, so do not get upset or argue with people who do not understand your Kingdom's purpose. Here is what I want to share with you, everyone cannot go where God is taking you. As you start the journey to your destiny, along the way you are going to discover who is in your corner and who is not. You will lose friends and even some family members will stop speaking to you, you may be shocked by those you lose. Just remember, as those relationships end, God will replace them with purposeful ones. Purpose relationships will help push you towards all God has for you. Do not seek to hold on to those who God is separating you from. Staying in relationships that don't support your mission will only stagnate you and prevent you from answering the call.

One of the hardest things I have had to endure while embracing my calling was losing the longstanding relationships, some who were my confidants. I lost all my childhood and early adulthood friends. As I matured in Christ, I understood that it was necessary for me to separate from them for me to walk in my purpose, because where God was taking me, they could not go. The things I did with them would not serve in my calling. I was transforming spiritually, and they were happy with who they were in the secular world. Now do not misunderstand me, although I no longer have friendships with them, they are not my enemies either. I would still give them the shirt off my back if they needed my help. God had to separate me from them because my destiny and purpose were taking me in a different direction. As you mature in your faith and purpose, you too will come to understand why certain people who you were once close to have no place in the assignments God has for you. By the time I was 30 years of age, all my friends were new. Now, my circle of friends is small and each of them have a spiritual purpose for me and me for them.

So now that you are ready to fulfill your divine assignment, you may be wondering where to start. Well, I always start in prayer and meditation with God. "Trust in the LORD with all thine heart; and lean not to thine own understanding. In all thy ways, acknowledge him, and he will direct your path " (Proverbs 3:5-6 KJV). I want to make sure I am following His will and not my own. I always ask God to make His will plain for me so that I know beyond a shadow of doubt that I will be doing what He wants me to do. When God tells you what He wants you to do, write it down. "Then the LORD replied; Write down the revelation and make it plain on tablets so that a herald may run with it." (Habakkuk 2:2, NIV). It is good to write down everything that the Holy Spirit reveals to you. I am a planner by nature, as I mentioned earlier, I keep tablets in every room of my home because I never know when the Holy Spirit is going to reveal something to me. As things are revealed and shown to me, I write them down copiously, detailed as possible. I also reflect on my notes and devise a plan on how I will approach my assignment. Take this book for instance, I wrote an outline on what I wanted to discuss, I jotted down numerous titles to entitle this book and envisioned how the book cover should look before I wrote one word. I also pondered whether to consult with a book coach for this project or not. I even wrote other streams of incomes that possibly could spin-off from this book, for example, future workshops, speaking engagements, and a workbook. As I mentioned previously, God does not always give you all of the information you need for your purpose in one setting, sometimes He gives it to you in pieces. That is because He does not want to overwhelm you. He sometimes gives you bite size pieces of information so that you can complete one part of the task before starting another part. Another reason why He will give you a piece of the assignment is to see if you will be faithful to trust Him to lead you and follow instructions. Whatever His reason, when He feels you are spiritually strong enough to complete your assignment, He will give you instructions accordingly.

A great example of God giving a small assignment in a bigger purpose is the story of Abraham,

"Now the Lord had said unto Abraham, Get thee out of thy country, and from thy kindred, and from thy father's house, unto a land that I will shew thee. And I will make of thee a great nation, and I will bless thee, and make thy name great, and thou shalt be a blessing" (Genesis 12:1-32 KJV).

By gathering his family and leaving the familiar, Abraham showed God that he trusted Him. He had to act in faith. If you read on throughout the book of Genesis, you will find, God revealed His plan for Abraham in pieces and not all at one time. In the same way, there will be times when the Lord will share minimal details of your task with you. Yes, my friend, patience and obedience are needed for the journey ahead of you. "But let patience have her perfect work, that ye may be perfect and entire, wanting nothing." (James 1:4 KJV)

There will be times when God will use trials to strengthen you spiritually. During those times you will still have to keep the faith, all while completing your assignment. Take Abraham for instance, he waited patiently on the Lord for 25 years before Isaac was born, enduring every test and trial that was thrown his way. He did not have all of the information, but he received portions as God saw fit to share. In the same way, you will be faced with times that our Heavenly Father will withhold certain information so that patience can have it is perfect work in you. Though we live in an instantaneous, immediate gratification society, that is not how God moves or operates. Everything is in His timing.

"Everyone had a first time doing everything they know how to do."

When those two conferences were canceled, I was disappointed and heartbroken. I knew my calling was to be a motivational speaker. During church service one Sunday, it was dropped in my spirit to host my own conference. After church services, while driving home, I asked my husband what he thought about me hosting my own conference. He immediately said, "I think that is a great idea, you should host it at the same hotel where you held your mother's retirement celebration." And that was confirmation that that was what

God wanted me to do.

I do not want you to be afraid of doing what God has called you to do because you have never done it before. Always remember, everyone had a first time at doing everything they know how to do. None of us were born knowing how to do the things we know now. Think about it this way, when we were born, we had to learn to crawl, walk, talk, and feed ourselves. We had to be potty trained, learn how to brush our teeth, and bathe ourselves. No one and I do mean no one, was born innately knowing how to do anything. We were either self-taught or formally trained. Do not be afraid of not knowing what to do or where to start. I told you I start in prayer with every assignment, during those prayers, I ask God for wisdom and guidance in the things I have never done or am not quite as versed in. Here is what I ask Him, *"Take my hands, work through them, show me what to do, how to do it, and when to do it. Take my voice, speak through me, tell me what to say, when to say it, and how to say it."* My friend, He has never failed me and by me praying that prayer, I am giving my hands and voice to Him. That's right, surrendering to Him so that He can work through me. So, it is totally okay that you do not know how to do everything that He is asking you to do. He will direct you to where you can learn, sending people and resources to help you acquire those things you need in order to complete your task.

When I was led to host my own conference, I did not know where to begin. I thought to myself, *Did I hear God correctly, He wants me to host my own conference?* I remember praying, *'Lord, please crown my head with wisdom and knowledge as I plan this conference. Please put the tools and resources, I need in place to plan this conference. Show me who it is you would like for me to invite to participate in this conference and above all, let everything I do and say be for your glory, In Jesus Name, Amen.'* After I prayed, I began devising a plan, writing it down and researching. I envisioned how I wanted the conference to flow. I wrote my plan and started reaching out to those who had experience in this arena. I remember reaching out to this young lady asking her if she could refer someone to me who could help me plan a conference, she replied she could do it. I asked her how much she would charge me, her response was, 'I will do it for free.' I nearly fell out of my chair. I began thanking her and telling her she was a God send. After that phone call, two things happened, I knew beyond a shadow of doubt this was what God wanted me to do and I then thanked Him for sending me the resource I needed to plan this conference.

One of the best things you can do for yourself is find a mentor and get connected to a network of individuals who are doing what you want to do or something similar. Be careful not to get connected to the wrong people, remember, communicating with God and following the Holy Spirit is critical to your success in fulfilling your purpose. You should connect with like-minded people and I am not just referring to business minded, I also mean like-minded in the spiritual realm as well. The worst thing you can do is to get entangled with someone God did not intend you to connect with. This could be very detrimental to you and thwart you from the mission. As I said in the previous chapter, as you grow closer to Christ, the more in-tuned in the spirit you will be and He will guide you letting you know when someone has an agenda different and contrary to God's plan. Purposeful connections are key to you, fulfilling your kingdom assignment. These connections will serve to help you in getting the tools and resources you need. I like to call these Godly connections because their purpose is to help to move you to your destiny.

You cannot and will not know everything – surround yourself with subject matter experts in the areas you are not as versed or experienced in. You would be surprised by those who are willing to help you get the information you need to succeed. Most are happy to help and if they can't often times, they will introduce you to someone who can.

Aside from a mentor, you may determine that you need formal training to do what God is leading you to do. I mentioned to you while separated from my husband, I obtained a graduate degree. Little did I know that experience and knowledge I learned were equipping and preparing me for motivational speaking. Every class I had, I had to present in front of the class individually and as a team with my cohorts. I even joined Toastmasters so that I could develop my speaking skills. Now, when I speak in front of audiences, I am not afraid nor nervous because I know how to write and deliver a speech with relevant content. My point is you may have to go back and get a degree or formal training to acquire the knowledge and skill needed to serve in your purpose, whether it is culinary school, nursing school, or even a course in graphic designing. If that is what you need for your kingdom assignment, do not be deterred in obtaining it. God will give you the fortitude to complete your schooling or training. Even now, I have to take a certification course for my next assignment and I am excited to do it because I know that this certification will help me serve in my purpose, which ultimately will benefit the kingdom.

Writing a plan and implementing it can be a daunting task. It requires thought, strategy, and precision. Take it from me, you will get used to it. You might even have to tweak your plan along the way, but do not be alarmed. As long as you stay connected with Christ, you cannot fail. Going back to the planning stage of my first conference, there were many nights I researched and reached out to others for guidance and/or advice. I wanted to ensure I was not leaving anything out. I solicited the help of my prayer partners, who kept me focused on the goal. They were instrumental in brainstorming ideas, keeping me organized, and praying for me.

Think about your gifts and how they will serve you moving forward in your purpose. How will you finance what it is God is calling you to do if there is a cost associated with your purpose? For instance, hosting a conference had several expenditures associated with it. I needed a location, food for the attendees, advertising, items for the swag bag, all of which had a cost associated with them. You must determine what costs are associated with your purpose, if any. For instance, writing this book, I hired a book coach, I formed a motivational speaking company, and hired a brand and marketing team to build the website to market me. Each of these things have costs associated with them and you will have to map out how to get things done and strategize how you will pay for these things. But just know, God will never give you an assignment without setting aside the provisions you need to complete it.

Planning your debut is exciting but there is much work involved too. I encourage you to pray, seeking guidance from the Holy Spirit on how and where to start. Remember, God may not give you all the information in one setting and patience is needed in abundance. You may experience setbacks, have hurdles to cross and overcome obstacles, but do not be afraid if you do not have all the know-how about what is being asked of you. Rest assured God has you covered. Some of your gifts may even be invisible to you until you start serving in your purpose. We all had a first time doing something. Seek out coaches, mentors, and training to help you along the way, this will serve to help you develop your gifts and talent. Finally, write your plan down and everything you will need to fulfill your task. Think about who can help you with what you need and do not be afraid to ask for help. Remember, to ensure those you seek help from understand your purpose and support you. The last thing you want is to invite the enemy into your camp, that would only serve to deter and distract you from completing the mission. You can do this; God would not have chosen you if He did not believe you could do it.

Before we move on, answer the following questions:

1. Do I have the knowledge I need to start serving in my purpose? If not, what am I lacking?

2. Who in my circle/network can help me get the knowledge tools and resources I need to get started?

3. Do I need to take a class or just purchase books and research the internet for the knowledge I am lacking?

4. What partnerships do I need to form to get started?

5. How will I pay for expenditures? How much money do I need? How much do I have?

6. Do I need sponsors? How do I get them?

This is not an exhaustive list of questions. As you answer these others may come up as well. The intent is to get you in the mode of thinking in terms of planning and strategizing needs to carry out your purpose.

DESTINY PRAYER

Dear God, thank you for not giving up on me and bringing me back to you. Father as I move forward to serve you with my gifts, I will allow the Holy Spirit to guide me. Father, thank you for showing me my purpose. Help me glorify you in my purpose. Today, I submit to your will for my life and I am committed to serve in your kingdom all the days of my life. Here I am Lord, take my hands, work through them, and take my voice to speak through me. Lord let me not falter as I serve you. My heart's desire is to glorify and honor you, my Lord. Hear my petition as I humbly pray in Jesus name, Amen.

CHAPTER ELEVEN
NEXT STOP DESTINY

Give yourself a round of applause! This is the day you have been preparing for! The day you start your journey on the path to your destiny. You have cried, prayed, and cried some more. God has equipped you spiritually with what you need to move forward in your purpose. It is time for you to walk boldly in purpose. Everything you have been through, the good and the bad was for this very moment. That's right, I know it is hard to believe, but all the things you experienced and have gone through were to move you to your divine purpose and destiny. Romans 8:28-29 says, *"And we know that all things work together for good to those who love God, to those who are the called according to His purpose. For whom He foreknew, He also predestined to be conformed to the image of His Son, that He might be the firstborn among many brethren."* I know it seems as if those times were so far away. While it is true those experiences did cause you pain, it also caused you to develop spiritually in Christ for such a time as this. Let's look at the story of David for a moment.

David was anointed as a king during his youth. Shortly, after he was anointed, he fought Goliath the Giant. After he slayed Goliath, he started serving in the current king's army. This king thought David was after his throne and sought to kill David. But rather than fight to defend himself David fled. While on the run, David lost his best friend, Jonathan. All of these experiences were working in David's favor, shaping and molding him so that he could take his place as king just as God had purposed him to do many years before. It would not be until David was 30-years-old that he would be officially crowned as king (read I and II

Samuel). I am sure there were times that David wondered what was going on, but I believe David had to endure these things to be useful to the kingdom of God.

Use my life as an example. The experience of me separating from my husband has allowed me to minister and encourage other women who may be going through something similar in their marriage. I have helped countless women in their marriage because of this one experience. Yes, as painful and traumatizing as the experience was to me, it was meant for my good as well as the good of others. And look at me now! I am walking boldly in my purpose and you should too. Embracing who you are in Christ and accepting your assignment in the kingdom is very rewarding. Your heart will be elated every time you help someone, just as mine is when I encourage others. I get excited just thinking about the impact I am going to have in the Kingdom, and you should be too.

"You are on the front line in the Kingdom, which means you are in plain sight for the enemy to see and attack."

Accepting your divine assignment will open doors you never would have imagined being available to you, but humbleness and a willingness to serve will keep you in the presence of the Lord. Proverbs 18:15-16, tells us, "The heart of the discerning acquires knowledge, for the ears of the wise seek it out. A gift opens the way and ushers the giver into the presence of the great." I always pray asking God to let everything that I do and say glorify Him and edify others. This is so that I never forget what I am doing is for the glory of the Lord and not for my glory. I never want to forget that I am the vessel God uses, but the message is from the Lord. Staying in this mindset keeps me from becoming arrogant, boastful or thinking I am better than anyone else. Depending on what your purpose is, it could place you on a local, national, or even global platform, which may cause you to gain fame and notoriety but be careful, always remember why you are doing what you do. Always keep in the forefront of your mind that what you are doing is not for your gain but for the kingdom of our Heavenly Father and His glory. You must stay humble.

I am blessed to have two very good friends (prayer partners) who keep me grounded. If I get discouraged or feel what I am doing is in vain, I can call them. They pray with me, encourage me, and remind me that I am not doing this for myself but for my Lord and Savior Jesus Christ. I encourage you to surround yourself around those who will keep you spiritually grounded and covered in prayer. Your spiritual accountability partner should be someone who reminds you of the goal, is not going to let you wallow in self-pity, holds you accountable for your actions and prays with you during times of adversity. These individuals understand your purpose and have a role in helping your ministry. Again, I must reiterate, you are on the front line of the kingdom, which means you are in plain sight for the enemy to see and attack. The tricks of the enemy are the same and have not changed. If our carnal being is left unchecked, the enemy only needs a crack to infiltrate the camp, this is why the entire armor of God must be worn daily.

When you feel discouraged; pray. When you feel weak; pray. When you feel like giving up; pray. Even when you are excited in the Lord; pray! Do you get the picture? You should pray all day every day. This builds your spiritual muscles and keeps you grounded. It is extremely easy to lose sight of your Godly purpose and fall into carnal minded thinking because you wake up daily in a society where any type of behavior and lifestyle is accepted. However, there should be something about you and your purpose that sets you apart from the perfunctory of the world.

Your attitude, actions, speech, and demeanor should mimic those of Jesus and your accountability partners should be there every step of the way to help you stay focused and aligned with your divine purpose and destiny. "The way of a fool *is* right in his own eyes, but he who heeds counsel *is* wise" (Proverbs 12:15). Let me present another example of how having a spiritual accountability partner is beneficial to you and your purpose. Let's keep diving into the life of King David. One day he saw beautiful Bathsheba (one of his soldier's wives) bathing. He sent a messenger to find out who she was and invited her to come to him. Bathsheba accepted the invitation and they slept together. Shortly after their encounter, Bathsheba sent word to David that she was with child. To cover up his indiscretion, David sent for Bathsheba's husband Uriah, in an effort to encourage him to sleep with his wife. Uriah slept in the barracks instead of going to his wife. So, David devised another plan, he sent a message to his Military Commander, Joab ordering him to put Uriah on the front line in the war where fighting was the fiercest.

King David had a true friend (accountability partner) as a prophet and adviser – his name was Nathan. Nathan went to David and told him a parable of a rich man and a poor man describing how the rich man stole the poor man's prized possession. When David became enraged over the mistreatment, the poor man suffered at the hands of the rich man and asked who he was, Nathan replied, "You are the man", and told him what he had done was wrong (II Samuel chapters 11 and 12). My point in recalling this Biblical story is to reinforce that you need at least one person around who is a trusted adviser to you; who will not be afraid to tell you the truth, and to provide you with spiritual guidance. This person will always ensure that you stay aligned with God and on track with your divine purpose.

It is important to remember your why! Like me, your reason for serving in your purpose should be for God's glory. Remember, *"If anyone speaks, he should speak as one conveying the words of God. If anyone serves, he should serve with the strength God provides, so that in all things God may be glorified through Jesus Christ, to whom be the glory and the power forever and ever. Amen"* (I Peter 4:11). Though your purpose may be how you earn your income, that should not be why you do it. Being compensated is a byproduct of what you do, why you do it should be to please God. For instance, it brings me great joy to help others and I know by using my gifts for God, he is being glorified and I am helping someone as well.

When you love what you do, and do it with a cheerful heart, you will be blessed immensely! God knows our hearts and judges our motives by what is in our heart. If our motives are not pure, we will not be successful. This is why, we must have a true desire to serve in our purpose because if our heart is not pure, it is impossible to please God. Have you ever done something that your heart was not into? Did you have difficulty in getting started or completing it? Much like that feeling of dreading to get started or completing the same will be with this if your heart's not in it. You will find it difficult to stick with it even in those periods of trials and tribulations and trust me they will come. However, remembering your why will get you through those difficult days.

You are destiny bound and that is extremely exciting. Keep these things in mind, your past experiences served to get you to this place. God used those experiences to shape you into His own. In all that you do it should mirror the behavior of Christ. Everything that you do should glorify God and edify others. This is your why, never lose sight of it. Though trials and tribulations will come, keep the faith, and hold steadfast in Christ. Doing so, will help you get to the other side of life storms.

Before we move on to the next chapter, I want you to pray. Ask God to show you who your accountability person is and what role will this person play in helping you. Write down everything Lord tells you so that you will not forget in the days to come.

She Does Not Live Here Anymore

That person who sought to try to understand why she was never good enough while seeking validation from a man. The one who lived carelessly in a world where she felt all alone. The one who was seeking happiness all on her own.

That person who was looking for love from him, him, and him giving herself foolishly to those who did not deserve. Not knowing her body was a temple that should be preserved. That person who constantly did things that slowly diminished her self-esteem.

She does not live here anymore; she has been redeemed.

The one who was crying out in silence for years to be saved. The person on the path of destruction traveling on the road she paved. The girl who would allow the opinions of others to mold her into what they wanted her to be. The girl who did not dare to say, "accept me for me."

No, she does not live here anymore, you see her address has changed. For the life she was living she did not want to maintain.

A man named Jesus knocked on the door of her heart one

day, He told her if she accepted and followed him; he would give her a new start. He washed her in His blood, freeing her from sin, healing her heartaches and pain working from within. As she transformed into a new person through this process, He hid His Word in her heart.

The person you are looking for does not live here anymore, she found joy and peace the day she opened that door.

No, she does not live here anymore, the day she accepted Christ, He gave her liberty. She no longer seeks validation from man, because her Heavenly Father gave her affirmation and now, she follows His plans. Christ restored her self-esteem, made her whole, and set-up His home in her temple.

No, she does not live here anymore, the person you seek you will not find. Because the day she opened the door and accepted Christ, she left that broken person behind.

CHAPTER TWELVE
PUTTING IT ALL TOGETHER

G ive yourself a pat on the back, you did it! You are well on your way on this purpose driven journey to destiny. You have faced your fears, taken off your masks, embraced who you are in Christ, and found your purpose. I am so proud of you. I commend you for your bravery as you embarked on this quest for spiritual freedom. Taking off your masks required you to transform your thinking and subsequent actions. "Do not conform to the pattern of this world, but be transformed by the renewing of your mind. Then you will be able to test and approve what God's will is--his good, pleasing and perfect will." (Romans 12:2, NIV) [1]

According to Phillippa Lally, and team's research, on average it takes 66 days to form a new behavior. Lally's research suggests that habits are formed by repetition and that missing an opportunity to perform did not affect the formation of the habit. However, Romans 12:2 tells us, we are to transform our thinking daily. This means daily when we wake up in the morning, we must center our focus on Christ and the spiritual business of His kingdom. On the surface, you might surmise that Lally and the scripture are similar. Although, missing one opportunity to form a new habit is not detrimental to the process; missing one day of transforming your thinking opens the door to the enemy to plant seeds of destruction in your mind.

Getting into the habit of prayer and staying centered on

---

[1] How are habits formed: Modelling Habit Formation in the Real World, Lally et al. - European Journal of Social Psychology – 2009

God daily allows His Holy Word to transform you into the Godly being He desires you to be. In order to overcome and withstand the wiles of the enemy your thinking must be transfigured into the ways of our Heavenly Father. There was a time when I would say just about anything, with very little regard for someone's feelings, not caring if I hurt their feelings or not. But when I gave Jesus every facet of my life that meant I had to give Him my heart, mind, and soul. More importantly my mouth! I could not just say everything that came to my mind anymore. I could not spew out venom tearing His children down, having little regard for how my words impacted others negatively. I had to be transformed by the renewing of my mind. Every day, I would quote James 1:19, "Wherefore, my beloved brethren, let every man be swift to hear, slow to speak, slow to wrath." Even today, when I pray, I quote Psalm 19:14, "Let the words of my mouth, and the meditation of my heart, be acceptable in thy sight, O Lord, my strength, and my redeemer." Why? Because I want everything I do and say to glorify God and edify others.

I cannot glorify God with a potty mouth or a mouth that says things to tear people down rather than building them up. How is that serving in my purpose if I do that? It does not, in the same way, you must not revert to the old person God has delivered you from. Find a scripture to stand on and during those times, when you feel you are about to do something the old you would do. Memorize it and recite it – it will help you break the desire to do those things you know will not aid you in serving in your purpose. You must let go of your old habits and form new ones in order to move into your purpose.

"Just like me, you have a direct line to our Heavenly Father through Jesus Christ."

Seek God daily. One of the things that I must drive home is you cannot make it without God on your side, even in the smallest details invite Him in. You have a direct line to our Heavenly Father, just like I do, through Jesus Christ. Talk to Him daily. Let Him know your concerns, express your gratitude, show Him praise and worship Him. I cannot express this enough, our Father desires to have an intimate relationship with you, He knows you by name. But if you do not seek Him diligently and let Him in, He will not force Himself on you and you miss out on a great opportunity to hear from Him.

We are all God's Cultivating your relationship with God requires commitment as serving in your purpose does as well. The only way you are going to know God's plans for you, what He wants you to do and where He wants you to go is to commune and converse with Him. No one can tell you the plans He has for you better than He Himself can. Do not be afraid to admit when you do not understand or you are not totally sure that you are headed in the right direction, He knows your heart anyway, but He desires to hear from you. Imagine your manager at work gives you a task to complete. Because it's new, you really do not understand what is expected of you, so you give him what you think he wants. Halfway through the project he checks on you and asks how the task is going and you tell him in detail what you have already done only to find out that is not at all what he wanted you to do. You have now wasted countless hours and have to start all over. Your manager then says to you,

"You know my door is always open, why did not you ask me for clarification?" The point I am trying to convey is that communication goes a long way and if you do not understand or you need more guidance or support all you have to do is ask and God is gracious enough to give you what you need to fulfill your purpose. He will always give you what you need to succeed, you only need to ask.

works in progress. You made the biggest step in seeking Him so that you could shed the mask and serve in His purpose. You worked on yourself, accepted Christ's lens of you, and embraced who you were in Christ. You have explored what your purpose is in the kingdom, accepted the call and invited the Holy Spirit to guide you in your journey to serving Him. You are devising your plan and gathering the necessary training needed to move forward. I am proud of you and you should be too. I know, how you feel – liberated, excited and are wondering if you can really do this. Yes you can! You have already come so far in this process. You will be fine, go ahead take the first step to your destiny.

I realize we covered a lot of information. From time-to-time you may have to refer back to a chapter until you are strong enough in your faith to fight off those thoughts of not being worthy or deserving enough. Those thoughts even try to overtake me every now and then, but I simply tell myself, "I am everything Christ says I am", and they disappear. Listen, you are not perfect, neither am I. If this road was easy, everyone would be on it and this book would not be needed. Do not get discouraged if you get off track. My advice is to get back up, seek forgiveness from Christ, and pick up where you left off. I know I have been there too but what I learned is that God is faithful.

Following Christ and living in your purpose is truly a

journey, and like most journeys, you will hit bumps in the road, have to be redirected, maybe even have to change your tires (mindset) and realign with God's mission for you. The most important thing is to keep your faith and trust in Him, never doubting that He is able to keep you from stumbling and falling. Utilize your accountability and prayer partner. I am in constant contact with both my accountability partners; they are my support system. They keep me focused, pray for, and with me.

Most of all, you have me – I am here to help. I am available to coach you, encourage you, and pray for you. After all, I went through these very same steps, overcame my fears, took of my masks off, and now I am proudly serving and walking in my purpose. There is not a day that goes by that I do not thank the Lord for rescuing me from me. One of the best ways to say thank you and show gratitude for what He did for me is to help you shed your masks, embrace who you are in Christ, and help you serve in your purpose so that you can help others. As I said in an earlier chapter, somebody is waiting on you just as you were waiting on me, because we are all connected in the body of Christ.

I wish you well on your journey to destiny. May you embrace who you are in Christ and discard your masks, never to put them on again. May God shower you with an abundance of wisdom and give you the knowledge and understanding needed to walk in the spirit as you walk in your divine purpose to your destiny. May you maintain confidence and humbleness, and may everything you do glorify God and edify others. In Jesus name, Amen.

ABOUT THE AUTHOR

L aSandra Collins is an author and motivational speaker. She is passionate about encouraging and inspiring others to see themselves as Christ sees them. Her mission is to build up and help others realize that they are everything our Heavenly Father says they are so that they can walk into their divine destiny. LaSandra's motto is: *"Every day is an opportunity to make a difference."* She believes this can be done through deeds and encouraging words.

LaSandra is the founder and owner of JIL Designs, where she sells spiritually inspired T-shirts. She also recently formed LaSandra Collins, LLC which was created to continue her mission in ministering to others. Her latest venture, Competitive Edge, offers career coaching in hopes to help others realize their career dreams.

Mrs. Collins resides in Spring, Texas, with her husband and youngest son. Together they have five children and three grandchildren. She is a member of The Church Without Walls in Houston, Texas, and regularly attends Bible study. Her hobbies include winning souls for Christ, spending time with family, writing, and traveling.

Some of LaSandra's work has been featured in the hit play, *"Faces in the Mirror."* In 2018, she released her first devotional book entitled, **"From A Christian Perspective: Encouragement for Daily Living."** Her articles are frequently featured in the monthly publication of the Faith Heart Magazine.

www.ingramcontent.com/pod-product-compliance
Lightning Source LLC
Chambersburg PA
CBHW072125090426
42739CB00012B/3074